Voice of Reason

Speaking to the Great and Good Spirit of
Revolution of Mind

Voice of Reason

Speaking to the Great and Good Spirit of
Revolution of Mind

by

Bryant McGill

THE

Paperlyon

PUBLISHING COMPANY

paperlyon.com / general@paperlyon.com

2015 S Tuttle Ave., Sarasota FL, 34239 / (941) 404-2663

ISBN-13: 978-0615615790

ISBN-10: 0615615791

First Edition

10 9 8 7 6 5 4 3 2 1

Book Description

Critically acclaimed by some of the world's top humanitarian, academic, and counter-culture icons, McGill's *Voice of Reason* is an illuminating, yet distressing plea for safety and freedom in a world of uncertainty, violence, and liberty lost. Sometimes eloquently poetic, other times harshly incriminating and shocking, McGill delivers a lovely and inspirational, yet thought-provoking book about the balance of mind and heart.

Voice of Reason is a wake-up call for a world in deep crisis, a world which is becoming a global battlefield, and where our poor relationships are increasingly based on self-interest. Exploring the true nature of violence, the destruction of diversity by monocultures, and the cancerous growth of unchecked, predatory corporate capitalism, McGill paints a grim picture of today's materialistic consumer life. Speaking directly to the heart of revolution, from Zuccotti Park to Tehran, McGill believes we must revolt against the endless manipulation and oppression of modern life, and reject the traditions of violence, which have made each of us agents of violence ourselves.

McGill explores many solutions to our cultural, political, economic, and environmental miseries, such as achieving greater individual consciousness and compassion, empowering youth, and restoring the woman to her rightful place, as the strong, loving maternal leader of peace and reason. As McGill writes, "The battlefields of life were first meadows and gardens. We made them into battlefields, and by the same power, we must release the dark spell, so they are meadows and gardens once again."

> "For a world consumed by a Culture of Violence, a *Voice of Reason* comes as a breath of fresh, positive air. The only hope of transforming the world from 'the tsunami of violence' is for each of us to Become the Change We Wish To See in the World. <u>Bryant McGill shows us the way</u>."

— Dr. Arun M. Gandhi
Grandson of Mahatma Gandhi

Bryant McGill is a best-selling author, speaker and activist in the fields of self-development, personal freedom and human rights. He is an iconic personality and cultural critic, whose writings have reached millions of people, and have been published in over 100 books and translated into 15 languages by publishers such as Simon and Schuster, Random House, HarperCollins, McGraw Hill and Writer's Digest.

Contents

Introduction by Susaye Greene

I cannot remember a time when I was not in show business. As a youngster, I did commercials in New York City, I experienced the rarefied air of Professional Children's School, where professional showbiz kids, ballet dancers, singers, actors and musicians could work during the day, and still get their college-preparatory education. Later, the *High School of Performing Arts* (which the movie and TV show *Fame* were fashioned after), where I majored in drama, after attending public elementary and junior high schools on Long Island, the major part of normalcy I was to experience in my younger schooldays.

Show business has afforded me the blessing of traveling the world. As a teenager, I saw Italy, Germany, France, England, Scandinavia, Japan, most of South America and almost every city large or small in America. My spirit of revolution was born in the sixties, to the wild guitar strains of Jimi Hendrix, while traveling the world with Ray Charles. My rebellious cry was hewn from reading everything from Malcolm X's biography to Jack Kerouacs' road-traveler counter-culture adventures. I met people everywhere, and picked up on world culture. I found my worldview; I began to see through the eyes of the world. Even though I will always be at heart an American woman, I became a sister to the world at large and began to see the connective thread that unites all of us as a universal race: the human race, as a necessity of my spirit. From Brazil to Paris, I learned the differences and similarities of so many cultures and I grew into a woman honed by the women's movement.

I believe women's issues are important still, though in my mind, there is no longer an in-your-face women's movement, per se, but I think most of us know things will never be the same since the introduction of the birth-control pill. While living in England, I became involved in a marvelous English women's book collective. We read books that promoted equality: non sexist, multicultural, multi-language children's books, covering most pertinent subjects, called Letterbox Library. They had a profound effect on me, showing me how women of differing backgrounds could truly and heartily share their views, and affect the source of education at the grassroots level. These scholars, mothers, teachers, English, Irish, Jewish, Jamaican, with different upbringings, made me face what the world is with such a broad perspective, through children's books for all ages. We read baby books to older teenage books. They were sold to schools, and to individuals. They continue their work today and are a great and far-reaching influence in English modern education.

My view of women around the world changed at that time, making me realize how important the woman's voice is as nurturer, educator, and planner of the future. But it was my own mother who said to me, "You can do anything you choose, be anything you want, reach the stars and learn infinitely." The grace to accept all people, to share the knowledge of my talent and experience, came from her. She taught me to know the power of my thoughts and that they are mine to wield as powerful actions.

When I met Bryant McGill, it was as if we had always known each other. Being able to see the effect he has on others with his words opened my eyes to a new way of looking at words and actions. I have seen him go through a great personal change on many levels, but his words continue to ring with such commanding truth, that it is impossible to ignore the strength and wisdom coming through him.

His "Voice of Reason" is a bell ringing to the sound of silent screaming: a wake-up call to a generation crying out for help. Without this kind of hue and cry, we may simply erase ourselves out of existence. The rare man who sees with extreme clarity, and peels back the layers of humanity for us to see clearly, is more than a welcome blessing during these extraordinary times. Bryant McGill is such a man.

Few have such a daring and bold sense of destiny, and only a few times in our lives are events lined up consciously, to show us what the possibilities of our goodness can be. In these treacherous times, where the fruits of caring are callously cast aside, we ask ourselves, "How can we survive? How can we remain human, let alone optimistic about our future? How can we retain the sweetness of our souls and the innocence of our childhoods?" And especially, "How can we achieve our dreams of peace in the futures of our children?"

The brave spirit of compassion lies just underneath the surface in each of us. Yet, our harsh reality strives to wrest that purity from us. I cannot imagine a more exciting time to live in—a time when our technology exceeds our expectations, and infinite choice lies at our fingertips.

We are told to embrace darkness at every turn, as the "new cool." Vampires, zombies and other nebulous creatures have seduced their way into our popular culture. Long gone are the days of manners and comportment. The internet has created a hotbed foundation of public opinion, with sometimes vile results—people hide behind false screen names to assume characters who thrive without grace, charm or manners. Bullying has taken on a new level of cruelty; people say anything they like, whether nasty, hurtful, or simply negative. It's every man for himself, full steam ahead, damn the torpedoes, my world, my opinion, me, me, me.

The ashes of our gentle caring are obliterated for the sake of any evil popularity. What is left is a hefty bitterness against our fellow man and our worldwide situation.

The simple act of listening is the beginning of change in our lives and the lives of those who have shared in the legacy of disenfranchisement of the spirit, because that act opens the heart to hopeful change.

Reaching out to our fellow human beings takes many forms, but clueing in to the need and the right to be heard is most important, because it takes us out of ourselves and into the essence of others. Which child does not need to be heard? Which man or woman does not need to be understood by others? We share the same feelings when we break it down; we all want the same things out of life: we want to be loved, we want to be safe and happy, cared for, cared about, listened to and understood, we want to be free to choose our lifestyles, whom we love. We all want to be educated, and work through our lives with passion and elemental success.

We cannot achieve these things without the simple confidence that comes from living our lives fully aware of others' needs. We think we stand alone, and many of us have been fooled into thinking we can succeed alone, in our selfish cultures. When we take away the trappings of status and competition, we are left with our simplicity; a race of human beings.

"Voice of Reason" determines and clarifies the goals of humanity, and helps us recognize the way forward. We can do anything we choose with our lives. The consequences of not choosing correctly are enormous.

—Susaye Greene

Artist, Activist and former Singer from the Motown Sensation, "The Supremes"
Singer and Songwriter for Stevie Wonder and the late Michael Jackson and Ray Charles

Preamble

There is something greater than any nation; it is the spirit which created the nation. It is to that spirit which this document speaks. These ideas are dedicated to providing a positive bridge of thought leadership, from the eternal spirit of good, to help the innocent, youthful mind of revolution arrive home safely.

∞

The *voice of reason* is that mindful and beautiful discourse, speaking for every heart's simple desire to exist in peace, harmony and cooperation, with our human family members at home and abroad. The *voice of reason* is immutably intrinsic, and exists as an innate feature of the good conscience, which is whispering to each person, at every moment, and is always speaking for the greater good of all, whether we are listening to it or not. The *voice of reason* is the beating heart of continuity of justice, reform of corruption, and the revolution of human consciousness, in those sacred and wonderful times of social change and evolution.

Where wise actions are the fruit of life, wise discourse is the pollination. Respectful communication under conflict or opposition is an essential and truly awe-inspiring ability of the modern human being's newly evolved social sensibility. It involves having the courage to listen carefully and respectfully, and then giving real and heartfelt consideration to what has been communicated. It involves reaching for deeper understanding beyond what was merely said and into what was meant or intended. It involves considering the greater context of the history and experiences that created the need for the discussion, over what may sometimes be years, decades or even centuries. This type of high-order listening is only possible with great intention, humility and magnanimity.

What every person or group wishes to say is important, even when we do not fully understand their message, and even when they do not fully understand their own message. This is because what we are really engaging in is a sharing of ideas, feelings and emotions. We are all thinking and feeling entities and we all have these wonderful and sometimes painful emotions within us, ever reminding us that we feel, that we are alive, that we are involved, and that we are inseparable from the great experience of living. We share profound interconnectedness with our natural and artificial environments, our communities, our created-nations, our institutions and with every person alive and to be born. Yes, we are all one in this great experience of life. What we do to others, we do to ourselves, and so it is essential that we reach for the highest place within ourselves, and afford every soul we encounter the wide and free passage they need to give birth to the dear expressions they feel are important. We must always strive toward our noblest behavior as good listeners by receiving messages with a graceful comportment, showcasing the highest state of respect we can muster. Even as the sometimes flawed, fragile and immature beings that we are, we can encourage and facilitate the mutual, free and respectful exchange of ideas.

The power of the idea is often overlooked, but if you think about it, everything is really an idea. A government, institution, company or even a society is really just an idea. They are constructs, or thought-forms of consensus reality, that only exist because we choose to support them collectively with the human resources of the heart, mind and hand. So make no mistake, there is no battle or engagement with any institution, company or government; it is always an engagement of ideas. Never lose sight of the fact that we are at all times exclusively dealing with ideas, and all ideas in a truly free society should always be open for discussion.

The systems of governance and community we create must hold many elements of life in constant consideration, the highest of which is freedom of the individual to live the life they choose in safety. Of course these considerations go beyond more than mere individualism, because the individual cannot exist outside of the many spheres of the deeply interconnected webs of life, so our solutions must also be organic and holistic. It is tremendously short-sighted when individuals, institutions, communities or other idea-constructs, fail to consider people during all stages of life. It is especially disgraceful when our created society fails to respond to the human indignities of not having our simple needs met, for we are all frail-embodied creatures, who at times suffer through injustice, abuse, illness, pain and misfortune. When a society becomes that insensitive and impotent, those dysfunctional or malignant parts must be engaged, and then transformed or eliminated to make way for more sensible and humane constructs. In other words, those constructs are bad ideas, which must be replaced with better ideas.

Respect is the lifeblood of progress, and the safe harbor of humanity's great aspiration—that all people have human rights affording them unfettered access to liberty and justice. Respect is that great spirit of good, which creates the beautiful space giving all souls the simple room to breathe. Every blood-soaked patch of soil in the world came from the grotesque attempt to surreptitiously or overtly control others by imposing selfish will over the broad consensus desires for safety and respect, and by failing to recognize universal human commonality. Any act of violence creates resentment and resistance, because humans were meant to be free. This includes passive violence, which is ubiquitous in today's current world construct we have chosen for ourselves.

Any being or group of beings seeking to silence the *voice of reason*, or ignore her nurturing will of protection, are traitors against humankind's deepest and most revered and sacred impulse—the desire to be free. All people desire to be free from the molestations against the soul of greed, violence, force, coercion, deceit and injustice.

Without love and compassion, nothing is sacred. No marketplace, free or otherwise, is good when it fails to consider the basic human state of needs at every stage of life. No political body is sacred, sustainable or under protection, which allows the exploitation of its people, or capitalization from the subdued life-force of its weakest members. No nation's flag is great or glorious if it flies over the weak and downtrodden, even if they raise and protect it out of misguided allegiance. No belief or idea is sacred, unless it treats all people as sacred. And no construct on earth will stand, that does not stand for the least among them, as their advocate and humble servant.

One of the most sincere forms of respect is actually listening to what another has to say. Do not make the mistake of thinking that you have to agree with people and their beliefs to defend them from injustice. Listening is just. Listening is the way. Listening is the beginning. The *voice of reason* is speaking to us all, and now is the time to listen.

The Current State of the Human Family

"In times of universal deceit, telling the truth becomes a revolutionary act."

—George Orwell

As far as the eye can see, we observe divisiveness, separation and isolation. Fear is the greatest enemy; the father of all suffering, and love is the only cure for humanity's great afflictions. Anyone who looks deeply and honestly at the world today is surely confronted with the grisly realities of human life on earth; realities from which most people try to remain unattached. The pain of humanity's most maltreated victims echoes deep within each of us, in the form of our shame or ignorance. Those who suffer are always there, pleading for help, and the *voice of reason* within each of us tells us to reach out and help. We must not ignore this voice, for it is the very anchor of conscience in the turbulent seas of suffering, which suggests there may still be something noble in the human soul. Listening to this voice is the last, thin thread that gives us hope that we are, in fact, not beasts.

There are too many problems in the world to enumerate: government abuses, genocide, starvation, human trafficking, slavery, economic and currency manipulation, usury, false shortages, resource hoarding, unjust wars, class warfare, arms proliferation, the molecular pollution of the biosphere, corruption, child labor, sexual slavery, rape and vicious crimes against women and children.

In the context of extreme injustice, some of the problems we face are of course more serious than others. Any serious reflection may cause some to realize that their problems even seem trivial by comparison to others. There are those who think distant problems do not apply to them because they seem above it all, but make no mistake, they are only momentarily in the eye of the hurricane, from which no one can escape through vain indifference.

So what is the state of the human family at large? The realities of human suffering are utterly monstrous. Even the "first-world" so-called bastions of prosperity, justice and law, are rife with corruption hidden in plain sight, which has been carefully crafted by the unwitting populace's hidden masters. Orwellian times of universal deceit are upon us, where every injustice is presented as solution and gift. It seems that everywhere you look, you see the same tyranny wearing different costumes; some more transparent than others, but underneath, it is the same dark and selfish spirit.

The overt crimes committed against people around the world are enough to send us desperately searching for the solid ground of meaning and sanity in an insane world, for both violence and murder are forms of insanity. What do we do when the world seemingly lacks the wisdom to live in the grace and peace, choosing instead to exist in a state of dis-ease? How can we break free from the chains which shackle each soul through the binding links of fear, greed and indifference?

There is no problem that greater consciousness and compassion, enjoined with positive resolve of will cannot solve. The *voice of reason* tells us that while great horrors exist in the world, we are all one, and there is still hope through love. Love and respect changes everything.

Rabbi Haim of Romshishok often began his talks with the following story.

> I once ascended to the firmaments. I first went to see Hell and the sight was horrifying. Row after row of tables were laden with platters of sumptuous food, yet the people seated around the tables were pale and emaciated, moaning in hunger. As I came closer, I understood their predicament.

> Every person held a full spoon, but both arms were splinted with wooden slats so he could not bend either elbow to bring the food to his mouth. It broke my heart to hear the tortured groans of these poor people as they held their food so near but could not consume it.

> Next I went to visit Heaven. I was surprised to see the same setting I had witnessed in Hell–row after row of long tables laden with food. But in contrast to Hell, the people here in Heaven were sitting

contentedly talking with each other, obviously sated from their sumptuous meal.

As I came closer, I was amazed to discover that here, too, each person had his arms splinted on wooden slats that prevented him from bending his elbows. How, then, did they manage to eat?

As I watched, a man picked up his spoon and dug it into the dish before him. Then he stretched across the table and fed the person across from him! The recipient of this kindness thanked him and returned the favor by leaning across the table to feed his benefactor.

I suddenly understood. Heaven and Hell offer the same circumstances and conditions. The critical difference is in the way the people treat each other.

I ran back to Hell to share this solution with the poor souls trapped there. I whispered in the ear of one starving man, "You do not have to go hungry. Use your spoon to feed your neighbor, and he will surely return the favor and feed you."

"You expect me to feed the detestable man sitting across the table?" said the man angrily. "I would rather starve than give him the pleasure of eating!"

I then understood God's wisdom in choosing who is worthy to go to Heaven and who deserves to go to Hell.

There are many worlds we can create. One world is nothing short of hell on earth. It is a place where the unlimited creativity of humanity has been bridled and abducted by fear, creating a real-life nightmare of cruelty and indifference so chilling that death itself has become a welcomed and kind benefactor. The other world is a world held in your hands. You and those who love peace are the keepers of the bright torch of hope, and the guardians of its tendril flames that burn in the hearts of every soul throughout the world, no matter how oppressed and downtrodden. Those who see the world through the lens of love are the true visionaries. They carry the vision for all who yearn in their deepest sinews, that all children would live in a world of limitless possibilities, where each soul could reach the heights of their potential to love, and to be loved. The only difference between these two worlds, that will ever exist —IS YOU.

Toward a Civil and Sane World

"Liberty is the soul's right to breathe, and when it cannot take a long breath laws are girded too tight. Without liberty, man is a syncope."

—Henry Ward Beecher

Take any concept you believe in deeply and say out loud, and with full conviction, that your dearest belief may be totally flawed. Say, "There is no doubt that I could be wrong." If you cannot do this, then you do not possess the idea, the idea possesses you. Change will never happen when people lack the ability and courage to see themselves for who they are. An intelligent person is never afraid or ashamed to find errors in their understanding of things. We must evolve beyond our limited thinking in terms of exclusion and inclusion regarding people. Human nature seems to drift so easily into, and hold so feverishly onto the insane mentality of intensely competitive, us-versus-them rivalries of black-and-white and good-and-bad thinking.

His-story is steeped in a dark misery that stems from the phenomenon of social identities, that arises from even the most trivial characteristics. These thought-forms of social identities then become the class war-platforms, from which privileged groups work for greater power consolidation through favoritism. This is how class, privilege and prejudice converge to become a master's heel of control on a modern slave class. These divide and control thought-forms are the basis of our deepest moral crisis.

Male and female, black and white, citizen and non-citizen, Christian and Muslim, Protestant and Catholic; it seems there is no end to the dichotomous splitting and oppositional thinking of we and us, versus they and them. People so easily embrace the thought-form that one nation is somehow superior to other nations. They invest in the false notion that somehow "their people," as a national collective or cultural identity, is somehow separate, blessed, worthier, more deserving and therefore justified in acts of moral indecency against others. Statements can be heard in every country on earth, of course some more than others, that our country is "number one" or "the greatest nation on earth." This insensitive and bellicose claim accosts the kind ear of reason as a piercing screech of national supremacism. It is that type of supremacism that leaves no room in the world for equality and justice; only equality, for just-us.

The most unpalatable of these phenomena is the patriotic blather and banter over appointed and anointed sacred symbols, such as historical mythologies, anthems, mottos, flags and victory remembrances. The ceremony, fanfare and hysteria over these idols points to a deeply emotional and frightening, nearly religious fervor of belonging, that at times even resembles worship. It is upon these spiritual, intellectual and moral deficits that master manipulators apply their craft to sway the hypnotized and unthinking populaces into further engagements of moral indecency for the exclusive benefit of so-called national interest—and to hell with the rest of the world.

The absurd view that other communities, religions, races, cultures, states and nations, are somehow "less than" one's own comes from an underdeveloped consciousness and low self-esteem. Prejudice and supremacism reveal that people do not possess a balanced framework of compassionate independence and self respect. We do not belong to any national construct, or group thought-form, but in fact belong to our great and beautiful world, and to the entire universe, as free and unique conscious beings. Prejudice comes from insecurity and its spiritually infantile need of belonging. Out of the hobbled spirit of attachment, and the insecure need of belonging, come the gross judgments against those who do not belong.

Through our shortsightedness, we find ourselves constantly in battle in the vast human theaters of conflict. From individual man-sized bug-tussles of intellect and thought, to city and state showdowns; then off to the high courts as word-filled cage-matches of law, and on to the general assemblies, like cultural thunder-domes of state, national and foreign policy—we are endlessly at WAR.

We have been conditioned. From the moment we are born, our minds of infinite possibilities are plowed, seeded and cultivated by every word, institution and sacred belief we hold dear, to produce a foul harvest of exclusion, apathy, brute domination and death. It is a rotten harvest, where good people are manipulated to spill the blood of their beautiful children, and lose their honor by abandoning their highest truth as compassionate beings. We hide among one-another, lost in the crowd of anonymity and collective culture. We huddle tightly together as cowards, protecting the ranks of our false collective identity from "less-human" intruders, when the only obvious and sane truth is that we are all the same human beings.

Nationalism is one of many examples of this form of collective narcissism, where the citizens possess an inflated self-love of "their own people," to the exclusion of other human beings, who are equally worthy of having the basic respect which must be afforded to all people. Nationalism a form of cultural self-centeredness, and as a collective thought-form, can only exist because the dominant in-group is itself comprised of self-centered and narcissistic individuals.

The offspring of nationalist thinking too often expresses itself in exclusionary and passively-violent legal policies, and then sadly, through militarism, which becomes manifest on the endless blood-soaked borders and battlefields of humanity's great failure as a humane species. This failure is often accompanied by religious fundamentalism, magical thinking and self-delusion, which have been justifications for some of the most horrific atrocities in human history. Ultimately, the greatest failures occur when we somehow allow ourselves to not accept that we belong to a broader group called human beings.

When radical inbred nationalism blindly serves in subordination to the plutocracies of international corporate-states, masquerading as so-called free marketplaces, the emergence of an oligarchy ruling-class within a state of neo-feudalism seems inevitable. The force of the bonds between these corporatocracies and their quasi-citizen consumers is so powerful, that even strong-armed imperial constructs of governance like America are squeezed out, dethroned and ultimately must also bow in servitude to the consolidated global fiscal state. This is one of the reasons the completely "bought out" by special interests, American left-and-right duopoly has become a sad and sick joke, like a real life Tweedledee and Tweedledum.

Sadly, many of the universities which are tightly tied to government and corporate interests financially fall in line to the tune of the power elite, and act as major components of the iron curtain of propaganda. No amount of propaganda can conceal the obviousness that wealth has consolidated and the government is profoundly influenced by those powerful consolidated entities. These corporate mafias use their influence to legislate more laws and policies ensuring that wealth consolidation continues in their favor, and that their society of criminals may continue operating with impunity. We must dilute and disperse all forms of concentrated power that refuse to be accountable to majority wishes. Corporate power consolidation is so enormous that even the government could be viewed as a small appendage of a larger corporate organism.

Rejecting predatory capitalism in America is a way to respect and honor America, because America was never designed to be fixed forever, but was meant to be fluid and evolving. The ignoramus crow of "love it or leave it" omits other viable options, such as staying and changing it. That is why people vote—for change—and that change represents the real spirit of democracy and the real America. People who have trouble questioning their own country often have trouble admitting fault in themselves, both of which come from insecurity and lack of humility. Questioning ourselves and our country is healthy and essential. From generation to generation, America should never be the same country. Even the Constitution itself, the DNA of the country, can be altered by the collective will of the people, making America a self-evolving and self-writing program. This evolutionary model resembles that of intelligence, life and change, not rigidity, stagnation and death. What do you desperately hold to: the America of the past, present or future? Life moves forward. The old leaves wither, die and fall away, and the new growth extends forward into the light. Progress is not about hating or destroying America, it is about loving and building the world, which can only come from healing our national dementia.

The mythology of freedom under capitalism for the average person is a con job, which is white-washed and propagandized through sentimental patriotic fanfare, and through the corporate hijacking of the symbols and iconography of patriotism, freedom, self-determination, and the virtues of small, hometown free markets. The markets are, of course, not small or hometown or free. These propaganda constructs are control-illusions maintained by the myth-makers within the media and marketing departments of the borderless, multi-national, corporate states, which seek to maintain the hegemony of their corporatocracies through stimulating endless consumerism by any dark means necessary. The means and methods of mind control, manipulation, public relations and propaganda have long been understood and employed, for example as with Edward Bernays through the psychoanalytical theories of his uncle, Sigmund Freud and incorporating the crowd psychology theories of Gustave LeBon and Wilfred Trotter. Among these accepted tools are using, cultivating or amplifying fear and insecurity within the public's emotions, to then provide a "solution." This action, reaction solution paradigm is a master tool for manipulation, control and conquest.

The character Arthur Jensen vituperates Howard Beale in the movie *Network*, with the following admonition about the dark economic and political realities of the world:

> You have meddled with the primal forces of nature, Mr. Beale, and I won't have it! Is that clear? You think you've merely stopped a business deal. That is not the case! The Arabs have taken billions of dollars out of this country, and now they must put it back! It is ebb and flow, tidal gravity! It is ecological balance! You are an old man who thinks in terms of nations and peoples. There are no nations. There are no peoples. There are no Russians. There are no Arabs. There are no third worlds. There is no West. There is only one holistic system of systems, one vast and immane, interwoven, interacting,

multivariate, multinational dominion of dollars.
Petro-dollars, electro-dollars, multi-dollars,
reichmarks, rins, rubles, pounds, and shekels. It is the
international system of currency which determines
the totality of life on this planet. That is the natural
order of things today. That is the atomic and
subatomic and galactic structure of things today!
And YOU have meddled with the primal forces of
nature, and YOU... WILL... ATONE! Am I getting
through to you, Mr. Beale? You get up on your little
twenty-one inch screen and howl about America and
democracy. There is no America. There is no
democracy. There is only IBM, and ITT, and AT&T,
and DuPont, Dow, Union Carbide, and Exxon.
Those are the nations of the world today. What do
you think the Russians talk about in their councils of
state, Karl Marx? They get out their linear
programming charts, statistical decision theories,
minimax solutions, and compute the price-cost
probabilities of their transactions and investments,
just like we do. We no longer live in a world of
nations and ideologies, Mr. Beale. The world is a
college of corporations, inexorably determined by
the immutable bylaws of business. The world is a
business, Mr. Beale. It has been since man crawled
out of the slime. And our children will live, Mr.
Beale, to see that... perfect world... in which there's
no war or famine, oppression or brutality. One vast
and ecumenical holding company, for whom all men
will work to serve a common profit, in which all men

will hold a share of stock. All necessities provided, all anxieties tranquilized, all boredom amused.

These rabid corporate leviathans have nothing to do with free enterprise or free markets, and they regularly decimate and lay waste to small towns, small businesses and their proprietors; often the very people who vehemently support and believe in the mythologies of freedom into which they have been indoctrinated from birth. Make no mistake; these so-called free marketplaces are not constructs of small town capitalism, where local producers and small businesses compete on a fair playing field, but more closely resemble a no holds barred death match of competition. They are global battlefields of competition, where well-meaning, good and honest citizens are in fact working in direct competition with child slave workers earning pennies an hour. If you are competing with slaves, then you are a slave yourself. This sickness of the spirit through extreme nationalism objectifies and dehumanizes those from other countries. The outrage of child labour would not be accepted within in the USA or Europe should it come to light, yet is acceptable in the name of commerce because of geographical and cultural differences. Under global capitalism, we outsource our moral choices when we outsource production to developing nations, where sweatshop labor cheaply produces the goods we so eagerly consume.

We have come to a low place, where it is somehow acceptable to outsource corporate and national-corporate losses through predatory monetary policy, exploitative child labor practices and literal war engagements, which are all designed to subsidize the debts and losses created from a mindset of greed, selfishness and the insanely unsustainable business models of unlimited growth forever. While this certainly seems to be the modus operandi of Western imperialism, especially as seen in America's permanent war economy, it also seems every other diverse political construct on earth has its own unique way of subduing the spirit of higher consideration and cooperation. These mindsets, at home and abroad, must be considered part of a dark mental illness. There is a self-destructive program running in the consciousness of humanity, and we must write a new program.

The current programs are domination, greed, forced territorial expansion, hoarding and resource appropriation for the advantage of one group, to the absolute exclusion of others. The ways we seek conquest and competitive dominance over others is violence against the high spirit of sharing, cooperation and human commonality. Our illness arises out of the perverse need for competitive gain, even if it means taking advantage of others through marginalization, passive violence and violation of universal human rights. At its height, our dark lust for competitive domination leads us to complicit acts of murder from-a-distance, through tax-supported militarism.

The greatest problem with capitalism as an economic system is when the privately owned means of production are operated solely for profit, and only within the battlefield of a competitive market. A kinder system of commerce, which has no name and is yet to be invented by the ingenious human mind would be more helpful to human beings, by considering a true profit to only be that production which benefits the greater good of all, and cooperation to be a higher moral principle than competition. This is of course not solely a problem with capitalism itself, but with human nature. It is therefore the consciousness of the individual that must be elevated and expanded to a greater scope of compassion, commonality, kinship and cooperation. We must rethink our present concepts of difference.

Most group distinctions are artificial thought-forms, that only exist because we bring them into being through choice. Our restrictive and judgmental ideas about difference, are based on lifelong conditioning and groupthink, and are perpetuated by consensus reality and mob mentality. Any intellectual recognition of legitimately perceivable groups, absent the goal of mutual improvement is ignorance and an exercise of useless reason. Class warfare, racism, sexual chauvinism, gender inequality, religious God wars, xenophobia, genocide and ethnic cleansing are all the offspring of artificial group distinctions, or unnatural emphasis being placed upon naturally observable groups. When we assemble any force of thought or action, not for peace, and without consideration for the greatest good of all people, and which does not amplify the immutable truth of universal human commonality, we fail tragically.

But how can we begin to expand our acceptance of human commonality, when every generation is inculcated in traditions of prejudice which are encouraged as normal, natural and healthy? State worship is an essential part of every government's command and control, from the tiniest banana republics, to imperialist hegemons like America. This is why nationalism, patriotism and national identity are continuously reinforced.

Edward Bernays argued in his book, *Propaganda*, that the manipulation of public opinion was a necessary part of democracy:

> The conscious and intelligent manipulation of the organized habits and opinions of the masses is an important element in democratic society. Those who manipulate this unseen mechanism of society constitute an invisible government which is the true ruling power of our country. [...] We are governed, our minds are molded, our tastes formed, our ideas suggested, largely by men we have never heard of. This is a logical result of the way in which our democratic society is organized. Vast numbers of human beings must cooperate in this manner if they are to live together as a smoothly functioning society. [...] In almost every act of our daily lives, whether in the sphere of politics or business, in our social conduct or our ethical thinking, we are dominated by the relatively small number of persons [...] who understand the mental processes and social patterns of the masses. It is they who pull the wires which control the public mind.

Nationalism as we know it, is the result of a form of state-sponsored branding. The national identity is a consumer identity. Like manchurian candidates, we have been made into manchurian consumers, who subconsciously buy when we are triggered by our brand masters. Every state's emblematic propaganda is worshiped by the consumer-citizen as a super-logo, a brand Juggernaut. Patriotism is merely deeply-rooted government brand loyalty. This national pride is the culmination of a lifetime public relations campaign of psychological mind-control techniques. These techniques involve an immersive theme-ride like experience of created histories, flags, symbols, icons, heroes, theme songs and repetitive pledges. National identity acts as a consumer lever to manipulate the emotions of the masses, for the purposes of power regulation and the fulfillment of agenda.

The existence of excessive nationalism is a symptom of a deeper problem in the collective consciousness, which is continually being exploited. The inherent prejudice in unnaturally-produced nationalism causes a form of cultural blindness, which prevents us from seeing the obvious ways we could co-exist in the world as a co-operative human family.

There is a grand union beyond nationalism which serves all people, and which is rooted in what is real, versus what has been created or produced. His-story has shown that nations and governments come and go, but people remain, and therefore people are the ultimate foundation of what is real and worthy of our collective recognition, respect and protection. Instead of narrowing our allegiances to only include our favored nation, let us sing an anthem to the marvelous human being. Let us fly the flag of sisterhood, brotherhood and oneness. Let us raise our hands to our hearts in the revelry and glory of friendship, respect and common decency.

The battlefields of life were first meadows and gardens. We made them into battlefields, and by the same power, we must release the dark spell, so they are meadows and gardens once again. Through our nobler thought choices, we must reclaim the physical and metaphorical lands of opportunity, and build peaceful gardens in our hearts, communities and throughout the world. The truth is now as it was yesterday, and as it always will be, that the world is—as we are. The outer world is a reflection of our inner selves. We must always strive to reflect the highest vision of ourselves. We must endeavor to create cooperative societies. We must throw out the old, fear-based thought-forms and evolve, and begin to live as higher beings of compassion. All discomfort comes from suppressing your true identity.

Our minds have been poisoned and our accepted beliefs are unnatural and artificial. Every person's true identity is beautiful, and much of the ugliness we observe in others was put inside of them by external influences. We all know the true nature of the human soul, because we have all looked into the eyes of children, and saw ourselves looking back. When someone is suffering, there is a deep, visceral reaction in the core of our being, a flood of empathy and a frightfully desperate compulsion to give aid. When we see a person in physical crisis laying with a broken body and their blood pouring out, our deepest, most urgent instinct is to rush to them, and put our hands upon their wounds and comfort them. When someone is emotionally upset and crying, nothing is right in our own world. This is our truest nature— to help others, and to protect and love them. We see this on a large scale in the aftermath of a catastrophe; the world population is deeply touched by the images of suffering, and many rush to help financially or in person, when there is a tsunami or earthquake.

When we see someone laughing, our spirits rise, and the laughter comes pouring into our own souls, and we find ourselves helplessly smiling. When we witness someone commit an act of kindness or selflessness, our emotions are stirred and we are touched by the high, noble spirit of what we know is the greatest truth—that we care about others, and delight in seeing others happy and safe.

When we see people without their basic needs being met, who are living in squalor and poverty, a part of us looks down in shame, with the quiet knowing that things are not right in the world. We feel shameful about these disparities in quality of life, because we know that there are enough resources for everyone. We know that when we allow abusiveness toward people, creatures or the environment, we abuse the one hope that we could be responsible, good stewards of justice and have high human comportment. The lowest human choice form is careless and selfish, but the high human choice form is the touch of graceful leadership toward all that is good and safe. The highest human choice of thought-form is love.

Lust for possession and greed has ravaged the soul of humanity like a great cancer, metastasizing throughout society in the form of a nouveau post-human, consumer hedonism. The dark war consciousness and pride have seized upon the weak, with great cynicisms and glib, soulless intellects, that grind away like robotic gears at what they despise and can never understand. Kindness is seen as weakness and intelligence worshiped, even when that intelligence allows unfathomable injustice and suffering to occur under its smart watch. There is no greater intelligence than kindness and empathy. Kindness is the supreme intelligence. Let your brilliance be expressed through kindness. If you can be kind to people, you will be a genius in this world. When we become acquainted with any person on a human level, even a great enemy, we begin to see that no person is really so different from ourselves. Wish for the happiness of your enemies, for if they are happy, they are your enemy no more.

The answer is of course greater literacy, community and compassion. The power of "getting to know one another" is so immense, eclipsed only by first getting to know ourselves. Meeting another human is always a sacred event. We must become reacquainted with our true human selves, and not the modern avatar of a "person": a commoditized, corporatized, homogenized, zombified, denatured, worker-consumer drone. Humans have become speculative commodities incarnate, with their life force as a gross product traded on the open markets. And like monetary cyborgs, our human resource currency is mixed and bundled with exotic financial instruments to the extent that no one really knows where the product ends and the human begins. We have lost our humanity to the decimal point. Through this financial coup d'état over the human soul, we have lost our purpose, and many people see no way to escape the endless manipulation and coercion of modern life, which controls us through the fear of "losing everything"; mostly created and false needs. The total commoditization of the natural world has placed a veritable lien against the spirit of nature, and plagued once beautiful cities with capitalist eyesores, such as billboards and advertisements, which now appear on cars, houses and even people.

The path we are on could lead to a frightening dystopian future. It is an ancient story being re-written by a new generation of misguided oligarchists, who have also lost their way on the beautiful path of life. In so many ways we are still in the dark ages, but there is light appearing over the horizon of choice and consciousness. People have moments of consciousness and epiphanies throughout their lives, but then suppress the realization. This is because the system has already anticipated the freedom seeking mechanism in humans, and a micro control coup takes place almost instantly because of deeply implanted economic and social fear factors. The system has endless contingencies in place to keep the monopoly game players moving around the board that was designed by the top-hat wearing monopoly makers. If you move your piece around the pre-scripted board, collect $200 dollars, if you break a rule, go to jail.

We must quit playing the game altogether, and obliterate the false avatars and personas which have masked and smothered our true identities. Almost everything a person thinks is a lie, and an assault against the natural soul. You are not who you think you are; you are someone else's ideas. You have been produced according to your primal appetites, and you are a product. Reach deep within, and reconnect with the essence of your being. Separate yourself from the lies and illusions which are not you. You are not your things, your titles, your status, your bank account, your IRA, your portfolio, your credit score, your degree, your intelligence, your feelings, your occupation, your town, your sports team, your nation or your religion. You are not even your emotions, judgments or your fears. You are something much deeper and much more wonderful. You are something that intellect and science can never even begin to fully describe. The joy and smile of even one child is worth more than the prancing intellects of a thousand men, for we are, that we might have joy, and be free.

Within each person is the miracle of a unique consciousness unlike any other in the universe. Within you, you will find everything you need to be complete. Within you is the power of unlimited creation. Within each of us is the enormous creator potential. We must seek together to address the good aspirations of people everywhere, for we are bound together through great commonality. There is a deep interconnectedness of all life on earth, from the tiniest organisms, to the largest ecosystems, and absolutely between each person, no matter their cultures or traditions.

Because of our interconnectedness we all know that extreme poverty and exclusionary practices are violations against the basic dignity of people. The vast and beautiful world is the home we share together. Nature is our salvation, not technology or the intellect. Technology can neither save us nor destroy us. Technology can only aid the will, thus it is the will and our choices which determine everything. Nature is the ultimate technology; a technology we are still too immature, arrogant, possessive and careless to care for responsibly. Rather than trying to master nature we should start with the basics of trying to understand nature, cooperate with nature and share nature's life-sustaining blessing with our brothers and sisters everywhere. There are enough resources in the world for everyone. We must stop treating the environment possessively, and as an expendable commodity. We must protect and share the world. Sharing IS caring. A great deal of struggle and sorrow in the world comes from misguided feelings of pride of ownership and possessiveness, versus the humble spirit of stewardship as common temporary inheritors of the great resources of earth. The world has been loaned to humanity by the universal powers of creation. To believe we own anything is a ridiculous notion. We only own our brief, ephemeral experiences, during a flash of an appearance, in a small sliver of time. When we leave this earth, then every property, thing and even idea—all that was us—is left behind for the next generation.

There can never be any real freedom on earth as long as people try to exert ownership over the natural resources of the world. Ownership is yet another of the endless forms of arrogance engaged in by the lower self. The natural resources of the world do not belong to any person, organization, collective, or so-called nation. We do, however, possess the opportunity to be kind, loving and considerate to others. We possess the choice of turning away from the lower self, and reaching for the higher mind. We possess a clarifying and self-defining moment of chance to give others the greatest comfort they can have during their journeys, while we are seeking comfort for ourselves. Let your greatest possession be the ability to let go of any possession, joyfully.

Who or what process put people on earth? From what source do natural rights come? If we choose to not argue about the process by which we came to be, we can absolutely agree that some process has placed us here, and that process exceeds the authority of any current human-created authority. Even when we humans create authority, it is an extension of some process created within us by the source, and so it stands to reason that the very same source-flow of authority is available to all people at all times. Our natural rights come from an authority beyond the petty rule of man. We are all equal!

Look at the sad and perverted system of property rights as defined under American capitalism by her founding fathers. It was a ruling class of white male aristocratic landowners and businessmen, who took it upon themselves to recreate a new feudal system, under which the drastic imbalance in the standards of living between the very rich and the very poor was preserved in perpetuity. Our new millennium capitalist world of the one-percent lording over the ninety-nine percent is hardly any different, when you think about it. Even today, real-estate ownership is the major divider between the wealthy and the poor; where landlords are as the name implies, lords of the land, acting as financial masters over a peasant class of renters. The government and laws define the rules, permits and codes for building and land ownership, in order to keep the monopoly game players' pieces moving around the board from birth to the grave, with property taxes ensuring that even "owners" are really just quasi-economic sharecroppers, serving the true lords of the land.

Since we are all free souls inhabiting earth, who really has the authority to tell another where they are allowed to walk, stand, build, sit or exist? This is the constant challenge to authority, which is ever being squelched and neutralized by the power structures that seek to maintain their control. As equal human beings with temporary time on the planet, which has been loaned to us while we are alive, where does the authority of ownership come from? Any person should be allowed to go, without permission, anywhere and at anytime, and should be able to breathe the air, look at a sunset and exist as a simple human being while residing on this earth. We all draw breath and life from the same source of creation. Each individual is born into life as a creation from the source, and as an inhabitant and visitor to this planet.

But scheming man, like a weaving spider, has made a snare into which each new person born is caught and kept for the remainder of their life. This finely-crafted trap represents the highest form of prison technology, for it is a prison requiring no bars, and into which people voluntarily submit themselves for life sentences. But the consciousness of humanity is resilient. No matter how deeply humanity has been induced into a hypnagogic state, the consciousness survives and has its own way of re-emerging in time. This is what we see happening today around the world, the sleepy eye of humanity beginning to open and see. Soon we shall be fully awake, and stand clear-eyed and tall on our deepest principles and values, which cherish above all the gift of life and freedom.

We must never forget that the world, as it is, is not a permanent reality, but is a temporary product of our choices as creators. We are sitting on top of a vast cultural and historical pyramid of accumulated misconceptions, lies and myths, built one on top of the other. Every symbol, word, concept, discipline and field is only a temporary rest stop on the highway of discovery. The highway of human possibility extends on forever into unknown territories, which have not yet been imagined. There are possibilities that exist beyond our present "knowing," and to see those possibilities, we must abandon that which makes us feel safe. Discovery requires courage and acceptance that we are not in control, and that the future is uncertain. The world is starving for original and decisive leadership. The world is starving for leaders who are not afraid to dismantle the sacred and precious beliefs, which hold us as prisoners of the past.

We all desire a safer and better world; a world with more harmony and goodwill. All people want to be safe and feel loved. The ethos in the world is changing before our eyes, and the time has come for us to take responsibility for one another. As the master creators on this planet, we can improve conditions for all and learn greater respect for others. It is a responsibility for those that see and have understanding, and choose to not be bridled by fear, to step forward and lead the way. And how does one lead? We lead by doing; we lead by being. The only way is to teach with love, which requires looking beyond what seems, and remembering we create with our judgements.

Everyone who has an abiding reverence for the sanctity of life wants to promote as much non-violence and safety for people as possible. We are the world, both the good and the bad. We are responsible for what we are creating. Even the cultural momentum which is sculpting us through propaganda and advertising was first our creation. It comes from us, and it is us. The full mantle of responsibility is on our shoulders, and the great thing about life—the most magnificent thing about being these sentient human beings—is that we have been given the power of choice. That is one thing that we do have is the power to choose. We can change the world one thought at a time, one child at a time, one family at a time, one community at a time, one city, one state and one country at a time. Let the change begin with our choices this very moment. You are creating through your choices, even now. Choose wisely.

Women and Children, and Rejection of War Consciousness

"In the problem of women was the germ of a solution, not only for their oppression, but for everybody's. The control of women in society was ingeniously effective. It was not done directly by the state. Instead the family was used—men to control women, women to control children, all to be preoccupied with one another, to turn to one another for help, to blame one another for trouble, to do violence to one another when things weren't going right. Why could this not be turned around? Could women liberating themselves, children freeing themselves, men and women beginning to understand one another, find the source of their common oppression outside rather than in one another? Perhaps then they could create nuggets of strength in their own relationships, millions of pockets of insurrection. They could revolutionize thought and behavior in exactly that seclusion of family privacy which the system had counted on to do its work of control and indoctrination. And together, instead of at odds—male, female, parents, children—they could undertake the changing of society itself."

—Howard Zinn

To fully understand the state of the human family, and the problems we face together, we must carefully look at the ways women and children are treated by men. Throughout the ages, society has emotionally castrated the male, in order to condition his consciousness to become capable of unnatural acts of violence and war. This war consciousness is purposely cultivated to guide the male away from the natural, healthy balances between masculine and feminine energies, and toward more unbalanced and detached psychologies. This detachment from compassion in the male is produced in him, so he can do the dirty work for society and its so-called national interest, in the form of social competition, militarism and predation. Mothers should be very careful what type of boys and men they create, or allow to be created. The artificial man, which is being created, is indeed a monster, and carries within him the dark and unnatural male war consciousness. The war consciousness is a living meme; a parasitic blight on the soul of human consciousness. The war consciousness is alien and suffocating to the untainted spirit-nature of women and children; its unique cruelty is the vile domain of male dominance, and represents the lowest part of the male energy.

Around the world, women and children are desperately seeking refuge and safety from violence, death and sexual assault, which exists as the gross offspring of the male thought-forms of sexual conquest, subjugation and need for domination. Until women and children free themselves from the ravages of the violent, male war consciousness, there can never be peace.

Women carry the heavy burden of caring for the literal and figurative future of humanity in every way: materially, maternally, and spiritually. The passive and overt violence waged against the women and children of the world must end. The world will change when women reclaim their power as the sane, nurturing hands of love, which are ever reaching to cultivate a world of beauty, safety and harmony.

Through honoring, appreciating and nurturing women, we set in motion a seismic shift which will lead to a new and healthy relationship cycle. Eliminating violence and fear opens the portal to empowerment and communications. This respectful flow of information enables constructive, healthy, compassionate, and wisdom-based nurturing of male and female children. It is women who bring forth the future of the human race, and those early years of childhood are shaped, for better or worse, by the experiences and conditioning of the mothers, who subsequently pass relationship models on to their offspring. The current predominant attitudes were shaped by our parents, their parents before them, and so on back through history. Yet, this ancestral habit formation can be overcome, and humanity will be transformed when this shift occurs.

We must turn our eye and attention to the root causes of this pervasive, brutish dominance, and work to restore the woman to her rightful place, as the strong, loving maternal leader of peace and reason. Assaults against women and children are assaults against any potential positive future for the world. The *voice of reason* cries out to us at every moment, and says, "the future is in our hands," and we must protect the women and children of the world by unequivocally rejecting the male war consciousness. To protect them, we simply must set them free from the cycle of selfish violence, which is endlessly waged against them—and they will, in that instant, become an essential part of the natural balance of leadership the world so desperately needs.

Violence begets violence. Much of the horrors that we are fed daily through the media could be attributed to the loss of a sense of belonging and partnership in couples and communities. In the past, and in some indigenous cultures today, the stages which involved watersheds, rites of passage in life, were observed and honored. This communal veneration towards puberty, coming of age, preparation for manhood, womanhood, birth and death, and the stages of life fosters mutual respect, and violence and intimidation have no opportunity to rear their ugly heads where respect is present. Finding ways in which to recognize and honor these life-stages would most certainly contribute towards a more peaceful and peace-seeking society.

But until that transformation is possible, we must be conscious of the profound violence presently affecting the lives of countless women around the world. The problem is so ubiquitous that one could say the fish does not know it is wet. We are all a part of a culture of violence that dominates every aspect of our lives. Present-day society is saturated in the degeneracy of subjugation, which prevents women from fully participating in society as social equals. How can any serious discussion of breaking the cycle of abuse be considered anything other than useless rhetoric, when even in so-called developed countries like America and England, women do not even earn equal pay commensurate with their equally-qualified male counterparts? What is it in the value structure of society that allows overt injustice to exist generation after generation, with people paying almost no attention to the obvious criminal disparity? What does this say about the society, and us as its members? If society allows this, what else does the society allow? These are the basic questions we must all ask. It is the socially determined norms and traditions of gender roles, which must be challenged, and challenged with vigor.

In nearly all countries, including America, the truth is that women have a low social status, and are considered inferior, if not consciously, then by the policies, institutional traditions and practices, which reenforce through action, the thought-form that men are superior. It is the totality of the woman's crippled status that quietly gives a nod of approval to further acts of injustice and domination. Too many women, especially in so-called underdeveloped nations work for unequal pay, and do so with very little resistance. This sad acquiescence represents the level to which the spirit of woman is bridled, broken and conquered. While economic inequalities may seem less pressing than physical violence, they represent a mindset of tolerance for the violation of fundamental human rights and the unequal balance of power, which serves as the foundation for greater acts of indecency, injustice and hateful treatment of women. These economic inequalities are part of the same habits of thought that underlie the true and overt brutalities committed against women all over the world. Even though physical violence may be more obvious and more vile on the surface than other forms of subjugation and inequality, the truth is that both are expressions of the same perverse philosophy.

These hateful and vicious acts of literal male barbarism include domestic abuse, rape, child marriages, female circumcision and genital mutilation, dowry deaths, acid throwing, and so-called honor killings. Ultimately, all of these crimes serve one purpose, and that is to keep the women from sitting at the table of conversation regarding the balance of power between genders. This is the ultimate male tradition. The deeply embedded game of "the boys versus the girls" we have all observed in the school yard continues to play itself out as the stakes are increased in the great game of life. It is in the venue of these highly-competitive life games that the finely-tuned and unbalanced male sense of competition and his artificial war consciousness are focused on the woman competitor, to obliterate her rights and suppress her highest worthy forms of female leadership. Since childhood, the male war consciousness has made a life-long study of the female mind. This study is similar, in almost every way, to the study of an enemy before battle, which is used to achieve a perverse victory of domination— naturally and almost subconsciously. The problem is that women, as a part of a cycle of violence themselves, create and participate in the cultivation of the psychological instruments of oppression within the male consciousness. These unnatural psychologies are later used against the very women in society who first nurtured and ultimately crippled the male during upbringing. This is because the males have been groomed since birth, according to the specifications of a sick and perverse society, to become instruments of war.

What then are women being groomed for? Women are controlled by men like a currency of the world. We all instinctively know that for many men, the world revolves around money and women, and the conquest of both. Often, men want money to get women, or to use women to get money, or both at the same time. Women, their looks, traits and sexuality are reduced to caricatures of value for appraisal, show, trade and consumption. We see this every day, the way a new girlfriend is trotted out in front of friends and family like a cattle auction, to the winks and nods of passive commodity brokers, who all have a stake in this female slave auction. As a part of their conditioning, women voluntarily prostitute themselves into the auction and groom themselves toward the highest exchange rate—tragically entangling their self-esteem with the rise-and-fall of these perverse valuations. Through the process of objectification, women have been reduced to dollar bills, tucked away in a man's billfold, and spent at his will.

We must embrace new frameworks of understanding that reject the angry, domineering, sex-driven male as an acceptable model. Women do not need a knight in shining armor or a Prince Charming to come to their rescue. The "Big Daddy" animus father-figure can be a man, lesbian female partner, community, government or any type of power structure, but one thing always remains the same: if you are a good girl then "Big Daddy" will protect and love you, and if you are a bad girl, then you will be unloved, on your own, and the monsters will devour you. However, "Big Daddy" the fear monger, too often is the monster himself. The archetypal "Big Daddy" creates many of the fear-illusions used to keep women feeling insecure, dependent, scared, helpless, worthless and full of restless despair. Love is the perfect safety, or the perfect weapon.

Women receive messages from childhood that they <u>may</u> be rewarded and protected for maintaining a childlike comportment such as being demure, obedient, passive and subservient. However, if she rebels through exerting independence, asking questions, doubting myths, and especially self-reflection, she will be punished and rejected. Of course, this father-worship and voluntary subjugation is not limited to women. Little boys and men seek protection and validation from "Big Daddy" in the authoritarian realms of intellectual, fiscal and social hierarchy, and through fraternity, government, military, police and other consolidated power structures. The great father will not save us, whether it be your chosen mate rescuing you and making you "complete," or a personified "Uncle Sam" saving you from terrorist boogie-men. We can only save ourselves through elevating our individual consciousness, by realizing there is already completeness within, and exercising as much considerate independence, respect and fairness as is possible. Both men and women must carefully consider the roles they play. Both men and women are responsible for creating and participating in the dynamics of their chosen relationships with themselves, their communities and the world.

Society's broken male so desperately needs to ascend in the balance of power by subsuming that which is being suppressed in women. The natural and untainted male mind respects and loves the woman and her magnificent scope of capability and creative gifts. The natural woman really represents the antidote to the great afflictions that haunt the world. It is the absence of her rightful leadership which has created such profound imbalances that the entire plane of human affairs is near the tipping-point of falling into a cultural abyss. The most urgent and immediate solution requires the women of the world to achieve greater consciousness and authenticity, to reject artificial gender roles and social expectations enforced by perverse social norms, and raise more authentic and less artificial men. It requires all of us to achieve greater self-awareness and consciousness, and develop more intolerance for the obvious and omnipresent injustices we all know are wrong.

It will take generations, great resolve and presence of mind to heal the deepest wounds of these painful maladies. The male-dominated systems know they cannot maintain their current power structures if and when the woman is restored to her natural and powerful state as a great leader and co-creator. The bondage upon humanity's great aspirations is largely held in place by the state of the woman in the world. Men can never have the true power they were endowed with by creation, until they respect and protect the women and children of the world. This involves men releasing unjust control, and having faith in the process of natural and healthy relationships, where the distribution of power is fair and the spirit of intense competition is tempered with great desire for cooperation and justice. When we try to control, we become controlled; when we release, we become free. We need to begin to see hyper-masculinity as the disorder it is, and not as a strength. We must unequivocally reject the male war consciousness by understanding it, exposing it and reforming it. We must strive for the fostering of a peace-seeking society. We must imbue our children with principles of the higher-self, principles which see all people as true equals, and above all, which are sensitive to the delicate and fragile balance of life.

The True Nature of Violence

"It is will that endows the animal with weapons of defense and with the means of obtaining its food; it is will too that endows the animal with consciousness and man with intellect, for these are weapons like any other contrivance for escaping from the enemy or securing prey. Indeed, intellect is the most perfect of all the weapons with which will has endowed creatures, for as the ink sac of the cuttlefish serves to conceal the animal's flight or approach, so intellect serves to hide the intent of the will and thus to insure its success."

—William Turner on Schopenhauer

To understand what a more sane world may look like, it is important to understand the insanity of violence, and the true nature of violence, which is seldom discussed. That is because any honest exploration of the nature of real violence has deep implications upon the foundations of the society in which we live, and this impacts how we judge ourselves. Modern society, the political body, the legal and judiciary system, the state of governance, capitalism and the very fabric of the society itself, including our religions and so-called morals and values, are institutions steeped in traditions of absolute and total violence.

Like in the animal kingdom, where every creature has its defenses and weapons, humans also possess powerful instruments for camouflage, defense and attack. For example, the tiger has its claws and teeth, the eagle has its talons, the bee has its stinger, and the ant has its powerful mandibles. What then is the weapon of man? Is it his lumpy fists or fragile fingernails? No. The chief weapon of all human beings is the mind. The human mind is the most powerful force on the face of the earth. It is the human mind that allows human beings to maintain domination over all creatures on the earth, though many are equipped with very powerful systems for predation and defense. Since the human mind is the primary weapon of the human being, it is also therefore the primary and most significant instrument of violence.

Sadly, most of the weak discussions and inane posturing over violence in the human world is focused on physical acts of brutality, and the inanimate objects with which people commit these physical acts. Physical violence, however, represents only a minority of true violence in human affairs. To understand the true nature of violence, one must only look at the primary weapon, the mind. It is when we look into the institutions of the human mind that the vast world of human violence begins to emerge as an endless tapestry of cruelty.

The mind is like a gun and our words are like bullets. When one understands that the mind and words represent the weapons, it is then that we can begin to understand that the legal arena is literally a bloodbath, which by common sense we always knew was true. People use words to do battle and to hurt one another terribly, tragically and even mortally. Stress-related death is well documented. Walking into any office building, corporation, trading floor, boardroom, government department, or courthouse can be like walking onto a blood-soaked battlefield. There are bodies everywhere and all you see and hear are the streaks of bullets racing by your head. You look over to the left and see your friend holding her neck as blood shoots from a clipped wound in her jugular vein. Everywhere you look you see empty cartridges falling to the ground as bullets fly in every direction. The bullets are the words. The words in the contracts, the words in your employment agreements, the words in the cheating fine print, the slanted words in your newspapers and on your television screens, the words of the insurance companies and the actuaries, the words in the courtrooms and the laws. The words coming out of the mouths of treacherous co-workers, gossiping neighbors, and capitalist storekeepers hawking their cheap dubious wares, without allegiance to anything beyond the bottom line of profit.

Once you understand that the master weapon of the human being is the mind, you will then see that violence is everywhere—true violence. Each person has terrible acts of violence being perpetrated against them in nearly every aspect of their lives. Pitted against the soul of every flesh and blood human are endless institutions, all enabled, organized and operating on the exacting and absolute definitive and deadly word. Words represent the thoughts of people and thoughts represent the will of the mind. The same violence that we see in the animal kingdom in the form of competition is what plays out day-to-day between individuals and institutions through the mind and the word. Yet, what happens in nature is no justification for our behavior, because we are animals of consciousness with the ability of moral choice.

The total objective of the violent system is to take a free human being, and convert that human being's speculative gross lifetime output into controllable revenue. Human beings and their speculative GLP (gross lifetime product) are practically traded like super-commodities—a pseudo, and perhaps even literal preferred stock of the corporation of the United States. The path of the common citizen is voluntary serfdom as a speculative commodity. This sophisticated nouveau slavery represents the supreme form of usury. First, because the profits from the labor are not fairly distributed to the workers. Second, because quality life has been reduced by placing people in stressful and artificial environments away from their families and communities. But ultimately, the current social contract we have accepted represents a supreme form of usury, because we use everything and everyone in the process. America and other "developed" industrialized nations have become like the executive hands, or middle-management orchestrators for a large international conglomerate, that could be called *Rape the Natural World, Inc.* (RNW). At RNW, Inc. nothing is off the table, from genetic manipulation and patenting of plants, to copyrighting DNA, the molecular assault on the biosphere, and using every natural resource and human hand, no matter the cost to create and concentrate wealth. If children's tears could be made into diamonds, corporate thugs would indenture children and force them to cry. This is what happens presently to children in the diamond mines and the electronic assembly sweatshops. How many people have to die before we are rich enough? The endless victims of the system exist in a perpetual tsunami of violence in the form of this economic enslavement. The violence inherent in the institutions, corporations and governments is without competition.

The homeless, street gangs, "thugs" and other mostly powerless people with legitimate anger concerning poverty and class, are commonly media and police targeted, and portrayed as dangerous, menacing undesirables. Young revolutionaries, students, activists and protesters are similarly portrayed as misanthropic juveniles and lazy ne'er-do-wells vandalizing public spaces. But too little attention is given to truly dangerous and powerful political and corporate thugs who loot, vandalize and burn communities to the ground every day, with the mighty stroke of a pen. The boardroom is the ultimate war-room, where history's most destructive acts of violence and aggression against human dignity, safety and justice have been strategically orchestrated.

Acts of economic war and violence in the deepest sense are commonly perpetrated against people with a "gentleman's" handshake and a smile. These villains hide behind a mask of legitimacy and integrity. Part of their illusion of legitimacy is achieved through the custom of costume, by wearing the official uniform of competitive business, the euro war-dress called a suit. These extreme fiscal bloodsport competitors are the top predator savages of the concrete jungle. These predators eat people's dreams, vitality and youth, along with their 401ks, retirements, savings and security; they eat their lives and their hopes for living a beautiful life. Executive savages who eat human resource energy and soul-joy, by feeding on life-force in these ways, are discomfortingly similar to cannibals, minus the flesh.

Governments potentially represent instruments of tremendous violence, both physically and by the word, or law. As far as physical violence is concerned, governments have historically shown themselves to be the most effective and deadly terrorist organizations that have ever existed, at least this is true if body count means anything. Corporate capitalism, unchecked by restraint and morality, quickly becomes a steady source of passive violence, which extends as far as its greedy reach gropes and covets. Capitalism places individuals into direct competition with one another, with their minds and words as their weapons. The objective of life under capitalism is to capitalize or realize a gain—materially or socially—over your competitors. To realize this gain one uses the primary weapon of assault against his environment and competitors—the mind. The mind is an awesomely powerful pattern recognition, problem-solving and strategizing computer, which is highly specialized at inventing clever ways in which one may achieve dominance and gain over those in the field of competition. It is in the ways that people are employed, levied against by bond, lured into borrowing money from so-called reputable financial institutions, educated, sold goods, and peer pressured, that violence is perpetrated against the common person at every step of life. In essence, modern consumer life is a form of extreme passive violence against all people. The problem of people not understanding the inherent power of their own minds, and not understanding the true nature of violence, combined with the irresponsible institutions of unchecked capitalism create the conditions allowing enormous injustices to occur. We find ourselves lost in a perfect storm of consumption, greed, fear, suspicion, treachery and violence in the deepest and most meaningful sense, to thinking and feeling creatures such as the human.

The character Arthur Edens of the movie *Michael Clayton* spoke about his epiphany, where he realized the inherent violence of the system as an organism that is destroying the miracle of humanity:

> Two weeks ago I came out of the building, okay, I'm running across Sixth Avenue, there's a car waiting, I got exactly 38 minutes to get to the airport and I'm dictating. There's this, this panicked associate sprinting along beside me, scribbling in a notepad, and suddenly she starts screaming, and I realize we're standing in the middle of the street, the light's changed, there's this wall of traffic, serious traffic speeding towards us, and I... I-I freeze, I can't move, and I'm suddenly consumed with the overwhelming sensation that I'm covered with some sort of film. It's in my hair, my face... it's like a glaze... like a... a coating, and... at first I thought, oh my god, I know what this is, this is some sort of amniotic — embryonic — fluid. I'm drenched in afterbirth, I've-I've breached the chrysalis, I've been reborn. But then the traffic, the stampede, the cars, the trucks, the horns, the screaming and I'm thinking no-no-no-

no, reset, this is not rebirth, this is some kind of giddy illusion of renewal that happens in the final moment before death. And then I realize no-no-no, this is completely wrong because I look back at the building and I had the most stunning moment of clarity. I... I... I... I realized, Michael, that I had emerged not from the doors of Kenner, Bach, and Ledeen, not through the portals of our vast and powerful law firm, but from the asshole of an organism whose sole function is to excrete the... the-the-the poison, the ammo, the defoliant necessary for other, larger, more powerful organisms to destroy the miracle of humanity. And that I had been coated in this patina of shit for the best part of my life. The stench of it and the stain of it would in all likelihood take the rest of my life to undo.

We live in a culture of violence. We have been trained by a culture of violence and we are all agents of passive violence. This is because all of our relationships are based on self-interest, discrimination and a perverse need for gain. The need for gain, and advantage over others, is one of the chief driving forces behind all human misery. We are always being forced to achieve some gain from others in order to meet our basic needs, or to vampirically feed our lifestyle excesses and greed. People have always had preoccupations with vampires because the concept has energetic roots in reality. The vampire is a cultural articulation of a creature or process we know exists in actuality, but we cannot fully describe or perceive. It exists just outside of our perceptive reach, but we know it is there, real and feeding on us and our energy. In nature, most prey cannot see their predator's attack until it is too late, and this is why we cannot see that which feeds on our fears and energy. Man's super-predator is camouflaged and hidden in plain sight. It is the system itself that is the invisible mega-predator which feeds on our life force. The passive violence permeates the ambient environment of human life in toto, and we pass our progenitors' dark traditions of enslavement forward to our progeny. We are almost carriers of the disease of our own servitude.

Violence is that which causes harm or forces unnatural change upon its victims. We are all artificial and have been unnaturally changed by violence and unwholesome conditioning. We all know there is something wrong with our culture, the state of our world, and with ourselves. Humanity has been institutionalized and we are all the products of commercial and institutional life. We are now born in institutions called hospitals. We are raised in institutions called schools. We are trained for institutional corporate life in institutions called universities. We serve in institutions called corporations. We exist under the master institutions of military and government. We die in institutions called hospitals or nursing homes. From birth to the grave, mankind is an institutional creature. These institutions have processes favoring efficiency over loss, and process over people. As children of the institution, we have all learned various processes and ways of behaving, consuming and producing. We have been made in the image and likeness of that into which we were born and raised. We are violence. Our children are bullies in school, because they are our children. We cannot trust our own minds, traditions and beliefs. We must reevaluate our needs and addictions to see that we have been unnaturally developed in the likeness of our cultural creator, and are predators. We eat life. Drunken consumption of unnatural goods, whether it be food, media, the environment, or other people and companies through "deals and acquisitions," accumulates within you, until you eventually become what you feed on. Rather than the limited concept of, "you are what you eat," consider that you are what you consume, and as an organism and consciousness, you in fact become a commodity and predator yourself. We become prisoners through unnatural consumption, because we must continue to feed to live. In contrast to this, consuming what is natural, good and untainted frees you, protects you, and realigns you with what is natural, peaceful and safe. By consuming what is good and pure, and rejecting what is artificial, you free yourself from being a commodity, and you then transform from a predator, to a producer and creator.

We must all strive to self-reflect and to reject violence in all forms, from the subtle to the overt. We must all seek to unravel the deeply-rooted conditioning which has perverted us, and attempt to heal ourselves and set our inner-truth free. Love heals violence and all its sources. Love only serves and does not calculate. Love gives without expectation, while hate carries an endless tally of debts. Hate controls everything it touches, but love sets everything it touches free. To end violence we must only look within ourselves, understand ourselves and evolve ourselves. Innocence still lives within our hearts and the child within each of us knows right from wrong. All violence demands reform, and all violence desperately begs to be healed.

But how can the cycles of violence be stopped when there are endless incentives to continue forward as things are, and endless deterrents and penalties for rocking the boat and not participating in business as usual? Most people can be and are controlled energetically, and physical violence is not needed. It is as though there is a static charge of oppression in the air. People know how to behave if they wish to be promoted up the ladder in society. They not only know what to say and do, but they are especially aware of what not to say, and what not to do. And this is how they live their obedient, oppressed and fearful lives.

But what happens when people are not careful and obedient? What happens to those who live dangerously by being true to who they are? What would happen if one day you decided not to play along? Are there situations where you would be socially penalized or economically penalized if you did not suppress your true self? Are there consequences for your honesty? We all know that this type of opportunism and careerism is commonplace; we have all seen it or even capitulated to it. The world is not fair, and often fools, cowards, liars and the selfish hide in high places. If there are consequences for honesty and defiance, then what does this say about society? What type of society uses coercion— which means persuading an unwilling person to do something by using force or threats; for example, the threat of homelessness, poverty, shame, no health insurance, or "losing everything,"—to suppress a person's true nature?

This is of course a form of passive violence; the threat of losing everything if you don't play along. If you tell the truth to your boss, will you be fired? If you speak your mind to your neighbors, will you be ostracized? Should you just sit down and shut up? If you are honest and free, will you lose everything? By being a free soul, will a perverse society attempt to execute your energy stream? Will you be punished materially, socially and mentally?

A prison is a place where a person is remanded as punishment for not following society's rules. It is a *penitentiary* where its members are not allowed to advance until they are fully *penitent*. These penal institutions are not just brick-and-mortar buildings, they are also invisible, energetic, idea-institutions, which have been built on every corner and into the very fabric of the society of mind. You must bow on your knees at all times before the ruling-class norms to show you are submissive. The *penalty* for not obeying, or being a submissive spirit to the ruling-class authority is applied in these invisible penal institutions. The penalty for not playing along is you will be socially-jailed from moving up the ladder, financially penalized, or whatever measure of control is necessary, commensurate with your defiance and disloyalty.

As beings who have been raised, educated and trained in violence, we are violence. This means we also self-inflict violence, because violence is our only way of relating to the world, to others and to ourselves. You keep yourself in check through violence, and that is how the invisible prison works. It is a form of self hate. The mind is the first level of the control prison, where your own thoughts are like a jailer, guard or a violent captor, which through time you have come to know and protect in a perverse paradox of self-imposed Stockholm syndrome. Society itself, including the marketplace of commerce is the second level of the prison yard, and the socioeconomic pecking order of the other prisoners governs the majority, keeping most people obediently submissive and in-check. The third level is the system itself, which wears a mask of civility, yet will quickly reveal its true nature in the form of raw, unadulterated and magnificently-purposed force of violence when needed to suppress any threat to its true grip of absolute control.

Any individual will quickly incur energetic, and even physical entanglements with the system, if they become too disruptive to the status quo, or to the existing state of affairs of the power structure. The power structure, which has an emergence quality of complex systems where the sum is greater than the parts, arguably exhibits an intelligence of its own. This intelligent organism wishes to preserve its dominance and existence, and "consciously" understands that the real venue of control is the venue of ideas. People who do not test boundaries unknowingly live under the constant threat of violence as suppressed beings. There is a gun pointing at every person's head and they do not know it, because they are obedient and submissive. But many have discovered that if you step just outside of the lines of expected behavior through protest or even espousing ideas— men with guns and nightsticks will quickly appear. The truth is they have always been there at all times, with their guns drawn and pointing at you. This is how we live at all times, with the barrel of a gun pointing at us. Step too far out of line, and they will materialize like phantoms before your eyes.

These phantoms are energy assassins, who come to arrest the energy stream of your creative emissions, and neutralize you as a threat to the establishment of control.

They metaphorically murder your energy. The machinery of government and its war apparatus acts as a double-edged blade, with one side sharpened for outer enemies and the other honed for inner enemies. The government holds its self-preservation as its highest imperative. The system loves to make public examples out of so-called "troublemakers" to teach everyone important lessons. A personified system can almost be seen sneering at its subjects and ordering them to keep their heads down, and to not make eye contact, or else! But we must look intimidation in the eye, and stand defiantly against what we know is not just. Nothing is more beautiful than freedom, and nothing more grotesque than its molestation.

A person is not solely their body; a person is also the unique consciousness within. The greatest crimes in the world are not committed against the body, but against the freedom of the consciousness. In this regard, the world is full of murderers, assassins and energy thugs. Since you are not solely your body, they do not come to kill your body, but rather they come to kill your name, energy and output. They kill your energy with audits, legal fees, politically-motivated arrests or propaganda against your credibility, character or morality. They understand the tribal mob mentality, and know how to let the mob do the dirty work of social stoning, through condemnation and ostracism. This type of murder is completely legal, but is nonetheless a great crime. To murder a soul's freedom and essence of being because someone does not agree with their ideas is barbaric, and yet this is business as usual on planet Earth. This is the name of the game— control and hegemony. Control is violence; cooperation is friendship.

The truth is that no vile usurper of freedom can harm you if you have nothing to lose. True freedom and power only comes when one is free of attachments, including the attachments of attempting to control outcomes. There is nothing more powerful and nothing more dangerously beautiful than a free mind. This is why so many great defiant spirits, who continued to advance their beliefs in spite of energetic attempts to silence them, were eventually physically murdered. But even in the shadows of physical violence, the real battlefield is the realm of ideas. The real violence is committed in the writing of history, the records of the legal system, the reporting of news, through the manipulation of social contracts, and the control of information. The real violence is committed by each one of us when we choose promotions over justice and popularity over truth. We are all a part of a food chain of violence which will never end until we reassess what is truly profitable to a society, and until we redefine our very poor relationships with one another.

The war for freedom is an information war fought with words, misdirections, distractions and omissions. It is an information war because people are basically good, and when they are in possession of the full truth, they usually do the right things. That is the reason information is controlled—because the free flow of truth is not always expedient for those wishing to maintain control. Begin to see the violence around you; begin to see the violence within you. Turn towards love, and become love. In the new world to come, let us only consider a true profit to be that which is for the greater good of all.

Biodynamics, Anarchy, Consumer Democracy and the Danger of Monocultures

"Western civilization, in spite of claims to support diversity, is promoting a worldwide monoculture—the same basic values, institutions and points of view for everyone—which it calls 'globalization'. Western commercial culture with its pursuit of markets and commodities eliminates all true culture, which is based on quality, not quantity. It creates a culture of money that submerges any true culture of refinement or spirituality, in which everything can be bought and sold, possessed or capitalized on. [...] The destruction of cultural diversity, like that of biodiversity, is devastating to living systems. The loss of cultural diversity does to human beings what the destruction of biodiversity does to the world of nature. Just as we are destroying our outer landscape of forests and wilderness, so we are destroying our inner landscape of art and spirituality. Our minds are as polluted as our rivers."

—**David Frawley (Vamadeva Shastri)**

The homogenization of our consumer culture underscores a profound laziness and a sad lack of creativity and style. From coast-to-coast, any-town USA looks like the same sprawling strip mall, from sea to shining sea. It is like a bizarre form of consumer-xenophobia. The machinery of mass-corporatization loves the lazy, closed-minded tendencies of ignorant consumers, who have underdeveloped palates for quality craftsmanship.

Craftsmanship exists in everything, from goods and services to vegetables, governments and even personal relationships. It seems we often timidly seek predictability and ease over adventure and effort. How we create the things we consume is very important because the act of creation yields by-products itself. Life is a constant consumption of our environment through our senses. We consume sights, food, conversations, products, touches, sounds, air and time. But as creatures with a body, we should all be especially concerned about the quality of air, water and food we allow into our bodily vehicle. As an organism there is nothing more relevant or sacred than what you put into your body. There is nothing more "meta-physical," in a literal sense, than food. Food is the ultimate sacrament. Food is a part of our contract with life.

We want *cheap* products, even our food, because of false resource scarcity created by certain elements in society. But you can't twist mother nature's arm for a discount, at least not without some consequences. In life, you get what you pay for, or in other words you get back what you put in— no matter the currency: tender, barter or time. People who think they can outsmart nature have a few lessons to learn.

We seem to love to dissect, organize and compartmentalize, and to exert unnatural order and control over what we perceive as wild, unpredictable and therefore dangerous. Because of the way we horde and control resources as lords over people, most of our greedy processes are forms of efficiency consolidation. Efficiency and so-called profit are the main objectives. Industrialization for the purposes of scalability of profit through economies of scale has limits and deeper consequences beyond the surface cost advantages.

The monstrous hand of control can be seen in monocultures of specialization such as assembly lines, strip malls, row farming, feed lots, chain stores and restaurants (feedlots for people), federalization, corporate cultures, racist gatherings, suburban tract housing McMansions, factory farming, mono-medicines, entrenched patriarchies, budget fashion and sweatshops. The industrial revolution assembly lines gave birth to the sweatshops and indentured child slavery; as they say, you may know a tree by its fruits. The sweltering white-head of the capitalist greed-boil can be seen oozing out brands like Monsanto, McDonalds, Coca-Cola, Starbucks, Pfizer, Walmart and the flag-waving USA mega-brand "War on Terror."

There is a real war, but it is between authoritarian, fear-based, profit-seeking uniformity, and freely democratic, anarchic, organic diversity; a battle between unnatural deceit and natural truths. It is a battle between the digital, synthetically-glossy Billboard Top 40, and the imperfect, analogue truth of brilliantly-flawed local live music. But ultimately, this is really a war between the forces of life and death, and the sacred expression of self-determination and freedom of choice. Monocultural forces want you to forget your childhood dreams, grow up, look the same, act the same and be the same, and this is why monocultures are bigoted and intolerant of those who are different. Monoculture hates diversity of all types, especially diversity of opinion, and is therefore the enemy of free speech and expression. Monocultures create mind-monopolies. Monoculture hates small towns, artists, artisans and colorful diverse expression, preferring instead a one-size-fits-all solution, which satiates the largest number of people at the highest profit. Monoculture wants you to forget that the joy of life is in the community of the village, where you can touch, taste, smell, feel and experience a motley potpourri of cultural vicissitudes. This beautiful village is where the real human family lives. The zombie brand-drones of monoculture live in the grey prison cells of homogeneity, dearth of the vibrancy of choice— standing in a cultural bread-line, just to stay alive.

You cannot mechanize nature or people. Natural life is wild and dynamic, not tame and obedient. We have all seen a small plant breaking through the concrete sidewalk— this simple but powerful visual metaphor illustrates what happens in any domain where we attempt to control nature. Like fools we tamper with the low-level rules of the complex systems of life for greater efficiency and control, and we forget that nature already has the most efficient processes we have ever observed. If we push nature too far we are going to get hurt, and arguably those repercussions are already becoming apparent in so many ways. If we continue to get in the way, the wild river of life may cut a new course, and more than likely, not a pleasant one. All dominions of control—

governments, corporations, foolish scientists, reckless capitalists and oligarchy overlords— beware; the collective mind of the masses is a great uncontrollable river of extraordinary power. The power of people and nature is the final word.

We need to be respectful and careful with nature and the environment. Environmentalism goes beyond corporate green-marketing gimmicks, beyond debates over global warming and beyond the irrefutable molecular pollution of the biosphere. Environmentalism is about life itself, because the environment is the space where all life happens. From the microcosm to the macrocosm, there is a total symbiosis between the environment and all its diverse inhabitants representing an inseparable physical interdependence. From the fungi and billions of microorganisms in a handful of living soil, to intestinal microflora forming the endosymbiotic relationships enabling human digestion, immunity systems, and vitamin synthesis— no part of human life is possible without the total environment. One could say that from the tiny microbes, to higher-order multicellular organisms, we are all in this thing together.

The inextricable entanglement of the total sphere of life as one entity demands we treat it with a level of respect we could only term, self-respect. There is no environment existing as a separate system outside of ourselves; we are a part of the environment, and the environment is a part of us. The biosphere is in a state of homeostatic balance, and its processes contain the distilled intelligence of billions of years of delicate interactions that serve all life. When we try to alter and control nature, we upset those internal regulatory processes and disturb the equilibrium. There are potentially dangerous consequences for irresponsible use of force and control. These concepts are just as true in the sociopolitical ecosystems as they are in the natural world. We must be kind and gentle gardeners with people and nature.

We should expand our senses and reason to make wiser choices that bring us in closer, yet more respectful contact with natural life. We must release control. Control is not humble; control is arrogant. We must heal the Earth with sustainable, biodynamic, organic farming, and reject the unnatural, monoculture plant concentration camps of the industrial era of force and control. All monoculture is inherently vulnerable; from plants in gardens to people in urban centers. When you unnaturally crowd animals, including people, into overpopulated and tight quarters, the incidences of diseases will rise. This has been incontrovertibly documented. Taking any plant or animal out of its natural, dynamic, and diverse surroundings increases the number of pests. This happens because the number of pests also become concentrated, as the number of natural pest predators diminish, ultimately requiring more fertilizers, pesticides or antibiotics to forcefully sustain the health of the unnatural monoculture. The simple fact is that livestocks and gardens become stressed and weak as a monoculture. The same can be said of humans, in regards to stress and mental health as it pertains to social mind-cultures. Social mind-diseases arise out of crowding people into limited choice-spaces of artificially homogenized environments. When you narrow people's choices to a limited subset of mass produced experiences, by removing them from the village of natural community life, and put them into monocultures of control, things start to break down. Unhealthy, degenerate and self-destructive viral memes start to breakout, commonplace depression begins to reach a low-boil, and anger and resentment fester like an infection that will not go away. People crowded onto corporate and social conveyer belts, like animals in the slaughter shoots of factory-farms, are all part of the same big massacre of natural joy.

When we identify diversity as a strength, we are contemplating diverse people, cultures, open spaces, natural organization, room to breathe, individuality, respect, creative freedom and dynamic access to the raw, unhomogenized life-stream of choices and consequences. We are talking about danger; the danger that your meal or coffee may not predictably taste the same in every city, state or country. The danger you may be offended. The danger you may even be hurt in the activities in which you are free to participate. The danger of freedom is real, but enforced safety reeks of a much more odious danger. Real life does not come with a safety net interwoven from the entangling threads of government and corporations. The real safety net of life is community, family and nature.

Wake-up! Think for yourself, be yourself and return to what is real. Free your mind and free yourself from brand slavery. We are not safer or more culturally enriched working at big corporations (for health insurance), buying the same products, drinking the same coffee, eating the same devitalized and poisoned foods, and swallowing the same political, entertainment and marketing propaganda. By bombarding each person with hundreds of thousands of commercial messages per year, and through generations of cradle-to-grave consumer conditioning and lifelong intra-cerebral media drips, consumers have bought into the notion that monocultures provide more choice. "Diversity" as a hallowed slogan repeated by minions of mono-consumers is Orwellian Doublespeak like, "war is peace" but which says, "conformity is choice."

The monocultural corrals-of-thought are forms of enforcement which create class-stratification through brand self-identification. Television and media act as corporate slogan madrasas that indoctrinate and collate future product disciples into obedient purchasing-classes. Oddly, the *lower-class* buyers see the "big brands" as more sophisticated, not realizing that locally-crafted products often possess the hallmark of real sophistication the higher-class shoppers crave. There is nothing higher-class than real craftsmanship, diversity, originality and the service of skilled human hands. A craftsperson's hands create authenticity and truth, honesty containing blemishes and imperfections. These inconsistencies are a signature of great beauty; they are unique and defining. Artisan variation is beautiful to the unique eye of the beholder. In contrast, franchises and machines create identical uniformity, for equally indistinguishable buyers.

Real life is imperfect and shows differences and variety, characteristics which are not favored in monocultures. The coveted perfect life is a created standard, which is purposely unattainable. The deceptive, glossy media images of faces, bodies and social lifestyles, make us hate ourselves so we will buy a solution to love ourselves once again. The conditioning advertisements make us ashamed of our blemishes, imperfections and flaws, but these so-called flaws are really our strengths and gifts. These images, idols and fixations on conformity and unattainable perfection make us illusion-prisoners. The very brands that promise us relief and personal freedom deliver the opposite of freedom; instead turning us into material junkies. They are using us, and in the process convince us to trade our originality and personal freedom for lives of economic slavery and dependency.

Credit card companies, pharmaceutical pushers, automobile advertisers, fast food hawkers, grocery stores and banks all market us solutions, which promise us we will be happier and freer if we contract with them through their offerings. Auto corporations portray their customers exhilaratingly perched on top of a mountain, rather than the reality of being buried under a mountain of debt. They seduce us with visual dreams of being free, and we end up surrendering our precious freedom for a fool's paradise. The master illusionists use these powerful psychological triggers to prey on the deep emotional longings for safety, happiness and freedom we all have. We see it with credit card commercials that promise to protect us from marauding barbarians, but they are the pillaging, new robber-barons themselves— a psychological sleight-of-hand to hide in their crime in plain sight. In reality though, it is just more lies.

One bank hijacks the orange as a marketing symbol and has the audacity to suggest we put our money in their bank, because according to their ad, money does not grow on trees. Of course the exact opposite is true. Wealth does not grow in banks, other than fiat funny-money, but real wealth most certainly does grow on trees. The food, fruit, nuts, oxygen, shade, shelter and habitat of trees have intrinsic, everlasting and real value to human beings. No matter what economic system comes or goes, food and oxygen will always be worth more than gold or any other fiat currency. Money and true wealth do grow on trees. Beautiful food and health are priceless.

Yet we continue to buy what we are sold (through conditioning), turning away from the life-sustaining, organic majesty of real food and towards illusionary, counterfeit foods, which fill us with pesticides, drugs, chemicals, dyes, sweeteners, transgenic GMOs and brain-altering excitotoxins. We eat from a chemical cauldron of witch-KRAFT, or any non-food in a box with pretty, lying images on the package. There is a disappointing, reoccurring promise we continue to see, where advertisers avow to deliver meaning and joy to the consumer, but ultimately they only deliver illness and misery. The truth is there is no happiness outside of ourselves. These institutions are criminal enterprises of deceit and ill-intent because they harm people and erode the gift of life and freedom. All of these misdirections, and clever marketing tricks keep us from realizing that the sources of real value come from nature and human resources, both of which we already possess. The folly of endless consumerism sends us on a wild goose-chase for happiness through materialism.

When people are treated like a product, they become obsessed with materialism. Modern capitalist consumer-life commoditizes people and "educates" them to become human products. A culture that raises and grooms people to be human resource products in a marketplace cultivates non-individuals who experience life through materialism. When people are treated as creators versus products, materialism diminishes. This is because the way people see themselves changes. We see the world as we are, and also as we are treated and seen by others, and by our environmental situation. With rare exceptions, the people who work in corporations, like those working on assembly-lines, are not producers—they are products. This is a distinction that is often overlooked. Human products see the world as a grand carnival of products. Being a human product, versus a producer, makes people feel powerless as ultimately disposable commodities. In consumer life we become what we consume—disposable junk to be used and thrown away.

When we buy junk, we become junk. A disposable society is only fit for disposable people. The loss of craftsmanship to mechanization, specialization and outsourcing, and the orchestrated suffocation of talented tradespeople has turned America into a sweeping, franchised wasteland of disposable goods. We make junk, we consume junk and we are junk. One need not look too far to see entire communities in utter shambles. Planned obsolesce has fostered cities that look like above-ground landfills. These landfill cities are full of transient quasi-gypsy renter-citizens, whose household economic lifeline is subsidized by Walmart through its international exploitation operations.

In the franchised pseudo-communities the stakeholders of local enterprise have been replaced with centralized corporate shareholders. The difference between remote corporate shareholders and the local community stakeholders is an essential distinction to understand. Corporate shareholders seek profits for their companies without concern over the profits and losses to the communities they impact with their goods. Corporate shareholders use their consolidated financial, marketing and political strength to disempower local small business stakeholders. This power play allows remote shareholders of infectious corporate franchises to seize control, and to influence from afar, the community's social, political and commercial structures in ways that sicken and ultimately kill the community. This death struggle is between centralized corporate monoculture and natural and diverse, local community culture.

Local stakeholders who care about their own community are the supreme antidote to corporate poisoning of the community by brands and franchises promising *cheap*, consistent and affordable goods. Cheap food and cheap goods are dangerous illusions which do not exist. In fact, once the long term environmental, energy, social and human impacts are accounted for, the so-called cheap goods are more costly than the naturally priced, higher quality goods from local sources. Cities that impose bans on franchises experience an immediate resurgence of community development, increased product diversity and overall revitalization, once the ever-grasping tentacles of the remote corporate beasts are severed.

The propaganda spearpoint of corporate conquest is often the promise of convenient, consistent and cheap goods and services. Corporations use brands as anchor points to sell predictability, which is psychologically favored. People like predictability and they have been conditioned and miseducated to only look at the immediate "dollar" cost of the products they buy.

Using an example of a buying a bicycle is very instructive. At Walmart or Target, you can buy a stylish-looking bicycle for a very low price. The employee who sells the bike is not a community stakeholder, but rather is a disenfranchised, paid agent of the remote corporate shareholders. As an agent of the company, it is not his job to consider the impact the products being sold have on the local community, or the communities where the products were manufactured. Why would an employee for Target or Walmart, who sells a "trashy" bike, care if that bike ends up putting a local business owner and true stakeholder in the community out of business, before it ends up in a landfill?

These bikes are actually made for the landfill by design. One executive of a bike and scooter company who sells to Walmart was heard saying their new line of electric bicycles only have a "life expectancy" of 2-10 hours. They went on to say that for their customers, the most useful accessory to buy is a hook, to hang it up in their garage, and that they are made for non-use, with a shiny, appealing look and psychological price-point designed to sell. The product quality only needs to be good enough to get it out of the store, and to use a few hours before abandonment or breaking. Once these bikes are taken into a local shop for inevitably needed repairs, the purchasers often learn that to repair the bike would cost more than the original price.

Cheap products destroy the communities where they are built from a social justice, labor, resource and environmental accounting, and then go on to destroy the communities where they are sold. Selling junk is like passing on a disease, where the seller is the original disease carrier, and every hand that touches the product is infected. This is the poison that runs through the veins of cost competition capitalism where the bottom line is the only concern, and the stakeholders have been removed from the equation. In this arrangement everyone suffers. The remote impoverished workers who make the bikes are inhumanly exploited, and the local employee of the corporation selling the dubious goods is perpetually hovering on the edge of destruction through economic enslavement at subsistence wages. As a purveyor of junk, this low-wage employee can only afford to buy junk, and so the demand for cheap product is perpetuated. The environment where the bike is made is poisoned, and when the bike finally arrives at its predestined landfill, that environment absorbs the last remains of a toxic chain of destruction. Irresponsible corporations who create and sell disposable goods destroy communities and people's lives. Companies who sell cheap disposable goods cannot have a relationship, which is not abusive, with their customers, employees or a community.

Selling and servicing quality bicycles is a noble and meaningful profession within a real community. Working with your hands and extending the life of quality products has a tremendous positive impact on the lifecycle of material resources. As a stakeholder in a community, a bicycle shop employee has the privilege of reacquainting people with air, breathing, sunshine, moving their bodies and the meditative experience and magic of motion through self-propulsion. That experience is real; you and your body, going somewhere. And when something goes wrong, the stakeholder's values and accountability are there to serve the relationship and resources, both of which are sacred. The relationship is of course always the central issue.

People have a tendency to separate the concept of product from service, but in reality service is just another product. Customer service is a purposefully-cultivated cultural product of a company. It is about relationships. It is absurdly impossible to have good customer service while destroying the economy and community where that customer lives. The first rule of good customer service is there are no customers. That is a fictitious made-up word and concept, just like most of the symbols of belief to which we ascribe. In reality, there are only people; people we help or people we harm. A so-called customer is a human being. In the context of cold-blooded capitalism, a customer is a disposable commodity just like the products to be sold, which should be used-up and then replaced. A customer in the context of a community is a human being who has a share in the co-creations of the relationship between themselves and the service or goods provider. Real community is defined through sustainable and considerate creative relationships, which seek to do no harm, and to benefit all. And therefore, what we often see today is not community at all, but rather usury, exploitation and suffering. It is only community in that we are all grouped together as we are being abused and used. Generations of distilled cost-competition capitalism has produced low-quality goods for low-quality people, in such a way, where the recent generation of children can almost be said to have been born into Walmart. We are a community of victims. We must turn our backs on these false corporate communities and reclaim our identities as co-creators in healthy, considerate relationships.

Being a creator puts people back in touch with their power and purpose, causing them to no longer seek their identity and purpose externally through materialism. As long as people are products, they will be obsessed with products. When people become empowered creators, or producers, they begin to think about the internal gifts they have to share with others. Creative producers understand value as something internal to give, whereas human products and consumers understand value as something external to get. Human products want products. Free human creators want sharing, people and community. Consumer life and present-day corporatism is a form of passive violence because it denatures people and turns them into disposable produce. We reclaim our power, communities and families by becoming creative producers. To end materialism, you don't merely reject materialism, you reject the contract of existing as a corporate slave and as a disposable human product. Materialism is an identity crisis.

When we do not know our true identity as powerful creators, we are susceptible to being used and manipulated. We believe we are the consumers, but we are the consumed. At the highest levels is set the standard example for how we should treat our neighbors and friends. The international financial organisms treat humanity as a flock, repeatedly growing and shearing economic wealth in an age-old process of cycles of chaos and order. Through a type of social natural selection, these intelligent processes have become stronger and more evolved systems of predation.

These predaceous, abstract elements, are far beyond the word definitions of international corporatism or imperialist capitalism. They are process organisms compelled by survival and dominance strategies, that only adhere to the unwritten and unspoken laws of the concrete jungle. In this sense the commonly decried institutions of imperialism, capitalism and multinational corporations become symbolic, word stumbling-blocks, which effectively keep us from understanding the nature of the parasite. These familiar words and concepts are hiding places for unknown, essential entity processes, which exist behind the words. When we say "corporation" over and over, the investigations into those problems stop, because we believe that we now understand the problem and its source through this identification. But these problematic adaptable systems exist in all political and monetary structures. The essential nature of this timeless predator has been with us throughout human history in nearly every civilization and cultural system. Is it an external enemy, or an enemy within? Does this phenomenon of selfishness we observe in governments and organizations exist in each of us on a smaller scale? To understand the true nature of this problem would require deep historical, cultural and epistemological probing to peel back the layers camouflaging this system. Fortunately, acquiring a full understanding is not needed to save ourselves.

Inside each of us there is a marvelous compass which greatly favors life, freedom and vitality. Our sense for safety and betterment is also a highly refined instinct; a process running within us at all times. This complex instinct knows how to make course corrections when we are in danger. This process is in motion now, and is whispering to us the guidance we know and feel to be true. It is our *voice of reason* telling us to be careful. It may whisper at first, but will shout and scream if it is necessary. Our *voice of reason* is telling us that revolution is in the air, and that life is beautiful, precious and worth protecting.

Revolution does not require you to live an extremist life of austerity by abandoning all brands. Consumer asceticism leads to a monoculture of deprivation, which is the opposite of diversity and openness. You are also not hypocritical if you use name brand products, while promoting brand advancements toward sustainability. Invest in ethical brands when you can, and include the local producers and services—what we could call smaller or local brands. You can best change the system by engaging the system to explore its strengths and weaknesses. This is how the power of choice works.

The personal revolution is the realization that the village and nature have had the answers all along. Therefore, turn to your community and the great earth for sustenance and knowledge. Become fallible and human again by living dangerously and stepping off of the assembly lines of unnatural life before it is too late. The simple things in life are the greatest gifts. They are all there waiting for us to realize their value and partake in their blessings. We do not need to change anything, except ourselves. Nature is the supreme cradle of life, and must be protected and treated with the highest respect and care. We must have clean air and water, and beautiful natural foods for everyone, everywhere. We must cultivate beautiful spaces, where communities and families are free to come together to share and enjoy the bounty of earth. Above all you deserve real freedom, but to have real freedom, you must be wild and free yourself.

Military Chain of Reason Versus Blind Obedience

"We are miseducating the young to believe that military heroism is the noblest form of heroism, when it should be remembered only as the tragic accompaniment of horrendous policies driven by power and profit. The current infatuation with World War II prepares us— innocently on the part of some, deliberately on the part of others— for more war, more military adventures, more attempts to emulate the military heroes of the past."

— Howard Zinn

Defense is a natural right. It is healthy to develop effective ways to defend ourselves. Considering the world today, it would be hard to criticize the organization of a well-regulated militia in pursuit of securing freedom and safety. Defense and personal sacrifice can certainly be justified, honorable and noble. The truth is that the military seems to presently be necessary because of an unfortunate number of psychopathic human beings who wish to obliterate human rights around the globe.

The need for a military must be viewed as an ugly burden on any society, and all sane people must wish there was no need for a military or the instruments of war. As a member of the military, if you cannot ardently proclaim that you wish the military did not exist, and do not deeply desire that there was no need for any military, then you cannot be a good soldier or a good and sane person. Any sycophant of the military has been seduced by the spirit of death, the destroyer spirit and the war consciousness, and must reassess their moral positions. They then must look clearly at the hierarchy of their government and its commanders, and contemplate the deeper motivations of war.

To bring the concept closer to understanding you could say the same thing about nuclear proliferation. While we have these terrible nuclear weapons as instruments of war, or some would say deterrents, any person in their right mind would wish that there were no nuclear arms on earth. Even the people who invented, created, service and deploy them must look upon these weapons with horror, fear and apprehension, hoping they are never used and wishing they never existed.

It is the same concept with the military. To love and proudly exalt the military is a form of madness, for the work of the military is a grim, dark burden which none should find gratifying joy in undertaking. War and militarism without a planned desire for their eventual elimination on earth, is war for the sake of war, and represents the repugnant war consciousness. The war consciousness as a living meme seeks only to selfishly propagate its own survival as an organism of destruction and malevolence. Any sliver of morality within the institutions of war reside in the imperative hope by the organizations themselves that they must one day be superannuated by cultural advancement. Our allegiance to morality should always advocate on behalf of peace, and serve a vision of a future in which the institutions of war are obsolete. Allegiance is a concept we must carefully consider, by asking, "allegiance to what or whom?" Our allegiance must always be first and foremost to humanity, beauty and innocence. The true spirit of the military and law enforcement should be for the protection of human rights, the protection of individuals from injustice, and the protection of innocence. The ultimate goal of the military and peace officers should be the safeguarding of peace. Absent this philosophy, these institutions can become hollow instruments of force, destruction and terror, especially when misused or misled by those with other agendas or moral illness.

Keeping in line with America's historic track record of imperialism and conquest, the Middle East is being disintegrated and reintegrated; it is being disassembled and refashioned according to blueprint. What is happening is one of the most egregious criminal operations in the annals of history. If there were greater transparency and Americans knew the bloody truth about many of its government and corporate activities, people would not allow it to continue. This is why the flow of information is stringently controlled or manipulated. The closer we can get every citizen to the blood, death and suffering of real people, through zero censorship in media, the better off we will all be. But largely, western corporate media is just that—corporate. Its independence ends at the fist that holds the dollar. Hard reality and truth often draw complaints from people living fantasy lives, and advertisers are lost. People don't want real, except perhaps the manufactured drama of faux "reality TV," which the mob loves and easily relates to because they are immersed in the created, petty dramas of their own lives. America is a nation of illusions: illusions in the media, schools and government, where the Iron Curtain of propaganda holds its citizens in a state of darkness and ignorant apathy.

Humanity needs heroic leadership from those who see all life as precious. Humanity needs leadership from a loving-strength possessed by individuals who see the broader commonality between all people. We need leadership from those who are willing to exercise judgement, restraint, compassion and sacrifice in favor of the highest spirit and bonds between people that extend beyond orders, divisions and borders. Truth, communication, transparency, compassion, peacefulness, empathy, community and love; these are the tools for reforming our culture of violence.

If you have been tainted and sucked into the culture of violence, which relishes the use of cruel power, then you are a surrogate hand of death and destruction, and you have become a predator and an abomination to the noble spirit-nature of human decency. Indifference, blood-lust and cruel apathy are the hallmarks of beastly and psychopathic tendencies. The *power of the situation* in combat, absent sane and moral leadership, allows untamed and impressionable minds to run wild in the fevered, grinning blood-sports of death by the destroyer spirit. There is a base impulse in humans, which when kindled and set free, will even burn-up the hand that set the spark. We must be ever mindful of these ancient lower impulses, and keep them in check with the higher evolved and love-seeking mind.

Morality is a leadership quality which cannot be mechanized, mass-produced and marshaled at will by any institution. Therefore, the best parts of the institutions of war are deeply in need of moral leadership, and are deeply grateful for those leaders among their ranks who possess those coveted characteristics. Contrary to popular belief, the military does not want machine-men who blindly follow orders, for those are the very type of men who, absent the soul of conscience and morality, would turn their war craft against the very hand that trained and created them.

The moral leadership required by all law enforcement and military involves the ability for an individual to overcome the power of the situation with clear moral imperatives, and if so compelled, to disobey any immoral or unlawful order. By disobeying immoral orders, that individual preserves the institution's highest rank—dignity.

In a pre-transitional world, while the apparent necessity of soldiering and policing arguably exists, those institutions are upheld not by those who know how to pull a trigger, but by those who exercise restraint and morality. It is the clear leadership of morality which keeps these institutions intact. It is the unconquerable humane individual acting according to the *voice of reason* within who is the true defender of rank and order.

Clearly obedience to orders is an essential characteristic, without which the military would lack the reliability to achieve its missions. However, soldiers must not follow unlawful or immoral orders, and are in fact obligated to disobey such orders. In the military academies officer candidates are taught that blind obedience is an undesirable characteristic. They are taught broad thinking concepts such as, "obedience includes criticism", "verbal expression of disagreement is part of this chain of reasoning," and that criticism is not a "statement of disobedience or of disloyalty." As it turns out, Howard Zinn's reiteration of New York City Mayor, John Lindsay's words from a speech at Columbia University that, "Dissent is the highest form of patriotism," appears to be literally true even in the ranks of the military.

According to the U.S. Army Command and General Staff College in Fort Leavenworth, Kansas, the publication, *How Much Obedience Does an Officer Need?* by Major Dr. Ulrich F. Zwygart reads, "Blind obedience can be subdivided into 'ollieism,' a subordinate acting illegally or unethically to get a job done because he wants to please his boss, and that of the 'yes man,' who—like Keitel and Jodl—the classical pair of 'nodding donkeys' are men who do whatever their superiors want, without further questioning."

Major Dr. Zwygart says, "Obedience is the normal case. Orders or wishes of superiors are to be followed as long as they are legal and moral." We can see here that obedience, as long as it is legal and moral, is what is expected from a good soldier. But what if the orders are not legal or moral? What would be the correct course of action then? General Peter

Pace, 16th Chairman of the Joint Chiefs of Staff, the United States' highest-ranking military office, reinforces Major Dr. Zwygart's concepts when he writes, "It is the absolute responsibility of everybody in uniform to disobey an order that is either illegal or immoral."

It is also very clear from the Nuremberg Trials that the excuse of "I was just following orders" is not defensible, even with "legal" orders, when those orders are not moral. However, it must also be understood that disobedience carries perilous consequences such as imprisonment or even death. Obeying and disobeying immoral orders both have consequences. This places military personnel in a very difficult position at all times—a position of great pressure. But from all of this we can see one very important theme continually reoccurring—the theme of morality.

So why is it that civilians who dissent on the grounds of morality by questioning some military actions are often condemned as unpatriotic and disloyal? This is especially close-minded, considering that even the military itself honors criticism as a high principle in the chain of reason. It seems that even the public suffers from a civilian version of the militarily unacceptable "nodding donkey." Sadly, resisting influence in the power of the situation is more difficult than it seems, and there is a tremendous body of evidence that indicate social psychologies that produce these behaviors, in the public and military alike. In his book *The Lucifer Effect*, Philip G. Zimbardo, Professor Emeritus of Psychology, at Stanford University, calls the "evil of inaction" a new form of evil that supports those who are the perpetrators of evil, by knowing, but not acting to challenge them. There are endless examples of this dynamic, from the torture of prisoners by American Military Police in Iraq's infamous Abu Ghraib prison, to the crimes during the civil rights movement, and even in our daily lives at our workplaces through unscrupulous corporate activity.

If only every police officer and soldier had the courage to think critically, to feel with compassion and to make moral choices by listening to their own *voice of reason* within. After all, police officers and soldiers do possess courage. Their job requires it, for they risk their lives every time they go to work. The important thing they need to do is ensure they direct their courage in the right direction. To risk one's life for the sake of others is heroic, but to risk one's life in the support of maleficence is villainy. In the final analysis, history will judge those who stand defiantly against all forms of injustice as the true heroes, and it will condemn those whose blind obedience allowed innocent people to be harmed.

Question everything, always. In the movie *Good Will Hunting*, Matt Damon's character, Will Hunting, answers N.S.A. Agent, Bruce Hunter's challenge, "the way I see it, the question isn't, why should you work for the N.S.A., the question is why shouldn't you?"

> Why shouldn't I work for the N.S.A.... that's a tough one. But I'll take a shot. Say I'm working at N.S.A. and somebody puts a code on my desk, something no one else can break. Maybe I take a shot at it and maybe I break it. And I'm real happy with myself, 'cause I did my job well. But maybe that code was the location of some rebel army in North Africa or

the Middle East, and once they have that location, they bomb the village where the rebels were hidin'— fifteen hundred people that I never met, never had no problem with get killed. Now the politicians are sayin', oh, "Send in the marines to secure the area" 'cause they don't give a shit. It won't be their kid over there, gettin' shot, just like it wasn't them when their number got called, 'cause they were pullin' a tour in the National Guard. It'll be some kid from Southie over there, takin' shrapnel in the ass; he comes back to find that the plant he used to work at got exported to the country he just got back from, and the guy who put the shrapnel in his ass got his old job, 'cause he'll work for fifteen cents a day and no bathroom breaks. Meanwhile he realizes the only reason he was over there in the first place was so that we could install a government that would sell us oil at a good price, and of course the oil companies use the little skirmish over there to scare up domestic oil prices—a cute little ancillary benefit for them, but it ain't helping my buddy at two-fifty a gallon. They're takin' their sweet time bringin' the oil back, o' course, maybe they even took the liberty of hiring an alcoholic skipper who likes to drink martinis an' fuckin' play slalom with the icebergs; it ain't too long 'til he hits one, spills the oil and kills all the sea life in the North Atlantic. So now my buddy's outta work, he can't afford to drive, so he's walkin' to the fuckin' job interviews, which sucks 'cause the shrapnel in his ass is givin' him chronic hemorrhoids, and meanwhile he's starvin' 'cause every time he tries to get a bite to eat, the only blue plate special they're servin' is North Atlantic scrod with Quaker State. So what did I think? I'm holdin' out for somethin' better. I figure fuck it, while I'm at it, why not just shoot my buddy, take his job, give it to his sworn enemy, hike up gas prices, bomb a village, club a baby seal, hit the hash pipe and join the National Guard? I could be elected President.

It is unfortunate that so many who enlist in the military are from broken homes and broken communities. Recruiters sit like vultures preying upon the poor, oppressed and marginalized. They sell these young people on security, hope, dreams and the promise of a family, but war creates a false family. War and the military create a dangerous surrogate foster-home of community and purpose among its comrades, one that replaces the impaired version of community we presently have in our disconnected society. This sense of community is very alluring to its members who often deeply yearn for that absent loving support of family, community and friendship. The artificial family and "brotherhood" created by war is dysfunctional and hard to escape for the disproportionate number of its enlistees who joined having no foundation, family or support. Young and disenfranchised people who desperately need to "fit in" are told that obedience brings honor and acceptance, which ultimately leads to a "place at the table." However, the hidden stipulation is that this obedience must never be questioned. "Father knows best" is the silent message delivered to these loved-starved soldiers. The price of admission into this special community is the destruction of the heart and the suffocation of critical thinking and reason. Too often, when injured or emotionally debilitated in combat, these soldiers feel used-up, abandoned and unsupported by their nation and former comrades as they come home to a world that does not understand their suffering. In many cases it takes a lifetime for them to put their shattered hearts, minds and bodies back together again. Military personnel represent a special class of super-victims.

We cannot blame the military for being what it is, because the military of any country is a reflection of the country itself. A government, no matter how corrupt, unscrupulous or manipulative is a reflection of its people. What we presently see before us in society is a perfect reflection of who we are, both good and bad. Who are you? What do you wish to create today? What is your identity? What is your intention? Most people do not actually know how to think for themselves, and unfortunately that prevents them from even knowing it. You are not really free, and that is why you do not know what I am talking about. You are not who you think you are; you are someone else's ideas. One of the most important things you can do in life is to brutally question every single thing you are taught. The ultimate question of who we are is set before us at all times and answered with every action. Self-reflection, self-awareness, greater authenticity and consciousness expose more of the critical self-probing needed to escape from the layers of manipulation, conditioning and influence. Once you are fully divested from the prejudices and attachments, you can begin to visualize a world without fear, control and violence, and in that instant, you will be surrendering your personal role as an agent of violence.

In the future, all military needs to be voluntarily dissolved and disbanded by all nations. The sum of an organized military is greater than the parts, and as a whole, any military should be classified as a weapon of mass destruction. In a highly evolved future society, to the pride of its people, no military will exist. The most powerful WMD is a willful mind of defiance. Hold the dream of a world with no military passionately in your heart, and if you will not, or cannot, then the destroyer spirit has possessed you, and YOU are an important part of the great miseries of the world.

The Police: Crucibles of Society and Enforcement

"Revolt and revolution both wind up at the same crossroads: the police, or folly."

—Albert Camus

Police officers can become human crucibles of molten negative energy and stress; they can be vessels of toxic tension. They sit at the intersection of monumentally enormous pressures and stresses from all levels of life. Like an upside-down pyramid, from the heights of national and state legislation under corporate rule, the top-down weight pierces all of its pressure directly upon the police position. As some would say they are, "where the rubber hits the pavement"; they are the gun, weapon, hand of force, control, and the violence behind enforcing regulations and maintaining the current power-structure's definition of public order.

When you are dealing with a police officer, you are not solely dealing with an individual. Just as the police are trained to compartmentalize and separate you as a human, from the administrative handling of your legal "person" according to regulation, you too must consider what the officer represents legally and what "office" they uphold. A police officer is an agent of the system, and their occupation is a program of rules, which has been written to achieve a specific type of control. There is a hierarchy of control in place, and you, as an office holder of the title "citizen" in that structure, have knowingly or unknowingly agreed to subjugate yourself to this hierarchy of control.

The police occupy a rare and important role in society, and we, as individuals, must be wise enough to see the complete picture of the human, and the office behind the uniform. There are many interests that must be accounted for: the interests of the citizen, the officer, the human in the role of the officer, the community, the government and the society. This understanding requires us to look at the police with suspicion, sympathy, compassion and caution—but ultimately through the lens of human commonality and love.

We have all heard of the "Big Brother" police state; a so-called emerging totalitarian control grid that is seemingly becoming more restrictive with endless rules and regulations. Many people rightfully perceive the ever-encroaching government exercise of repressive controls, which are at times definite violations of constitutionally-guaranteed rights. As much as we are incensed when we see police brutality and abuse of power, and must absolutely fight against gross injustice when it occurs, we must also realize that the police need excessive and special compassion, at all levels, from evolved beings.

Police work is a job that produces constant tension and inner conflict. A police officer is trained to approach all interactions with the public with extreme caution. On duty, every interaction must be handled according to defined procedures and with the commanding demeanor and presence of authority. But the public expects a certain level of respect, personability, and even sensitivity from its so-called civil servants. For the officer, maintaining a proper balance of comportment between affable personability and the required demeanor of authority can create a number of complicated problems with potential negative consequences. To the hardened criminal, kindness can be interpreted as a weakness to be exploited. But for innocent citizens inexperienced with the police, being treated too authoritatively can be offensive, frustrating, and even a source of real stress and anxiety. Knowing how to navigate this nearly unwinnable interaction puzzle can become a constant source of stress for the officer. One of the ways officers frequently cope with this type of stress is by inevitably leaning more on detachment and strict procedure following. While detachment and following procedure may be the easiest way possible for the officer to walk the line of personal safety, it can nonetheless be extremely alienating for the public. Even worse is that procedure following cannot solve many of the real world problems with which police are confronted. In these cases, the officer must use personal judgment. But deviating from standard policy and procedure can create real liabilities for the city, the police department, and the officers themselves. This never-ending circle of social dilemmas keeps many police officers in a constant state of discomfort and stress. It is tragic, but many police officers have been greatly desensitized to the suffering of others by their job, and of course through their own choices and priorities. Many police officers struggle with depression and feel their job is creating a literal battle within; that is, a battle for their soul and their own humanity.

We must try to remember that when an officer seems insensitive, this is sometimes partly due to the highly-stressful situations in which they are placed by their job. The threat of danger is a constant reality for them. This is one of the reasons they can seem tense and mistrusting towards the public. Because the police serve a public who sometimes see them in a negative light, they receive very little recognition or appreciation for the work they do and the service they provide. This lack of support can make it an easier decision for them to "look the other way" when a fellow officer does not go by the book, or to just follow orders that are not necessarily in the individual's best interest.

In *Police Attitudes Toward Abuse of Authority: Findings From a National Study*, a survey of police officers by the *U.S. Department of Justice*, 52.4 percent of officers surveyed "agreed or strongly agreed that it is not unusual for police officers to 'turn a blind eye' to other officers' improper conduct." Further, "a surprising 61 percent indicated that police officers do not always report even serious criminal violations that involve the abuse of authority by fellow officers." If you are forced into an interaction with the police, the best thing you can do is to understand their situation and not give them any reason to stop caring about the importance of the ideals they possibly believe they serve. Be respectful.

But even respect does not always protect you. In the aforementioned report by the *U.S. Department of Justice,* "22 percent agreed or strongly agreed that officers in their departments sometimes (or often or always) use more force than necessary ... and 15 percent indicated that officers in their departments responded to verbal abuse with physical force." What this means is that any interaction with the police, even speaking to them, carries a real and documented danger that you could be unjustifiably harmed or even killed. These facts demand that all interactions with the police be carried out with extreme caution, and preferably with as many witnesses and recording devices as possible. But do not be overly cautious. It is a high spiritual truth that we create with our judgments. How you judge a situation, and subsequently respond to it, can alter the outcome of that situation. Always restrain yourself and do not show any form of aggression unless you are in imminent danger. When you are dealing with the police, your safety has to be your responsibility, and it would be foolish and dangerous to simply trust the process. Be smart and look after your own interest and safety with heightened awareness, a critical eye, and clear and calm communications.

Unfortunately, since 1856, the Supreme Court of the United States has ruled various times that the role of law enforcement officers is to only enforce the law, and not protect any individual. The motto "protect and serve," has little to do with their legal job obligations. Many police officers feel they have been reduced to little more than revenue officers who are not respected from the top or the bottom. They feel isolated and misunderstood, and can feel rejected and not embraced by their society. Police often already have, or develop difficulty expressing their emotions, and as a result are unable to process the toxic energies they are burdened with in healthy ways. This feeling of isolation is a terrible and hurtful place to be for any person. Everyone wants to feel safe, supported and loved by their own community.

While we should all look sympathetically at some of the challenges of police life, we must also understand that a level of corruption and cruelty does exist. There are certain behaviors that we should not embrace or accept. As a society of freedom lovers, we must have a zero-tolerance policy for acts of violence, abuse of power, intimidation, restriction of rights, harassment and even rudeness. The way we disagree and confront injustice is of critical importance. When fighting any great enemy; we must endeavor to not become the madness we seek to heal. It is essential that we be polite and respectful with our tones and words. You can say nearly anything you want to, if you do it respectfully. There is no enforceable law stating that we must agree, and opinions are still protected—IF you know how to comport yourself.

Some of the unfair uses of power by police are wretched and grotesque spectacles that should cause every aware person deep alarm and worry. The pseudo-militarization of the police, the US breakdown of Posse Comitatus, the erosion of constitutional protections against unreasonable search-and-seizure, and the careless disregard, and sometimes seeming contempt for rights of peaceable assembly and freedom of speech, has deformed and altered the spirit of trust in America. We have moved too close for comfort to a Taser nation, where the respectful communication and patience we expect from responsible authority has too often been replaced with quick demands of absolute compliance with no two-way communication; a lazy and brutish form of policing—a phenomenon very similar to poor parenting.

We all know it happens: abuse. There is no doubt. We can all see an escalation of tension, pressure, force and lack of understanding and empathy. We all have a responsibility to resist indecent treatment of all people. Police and citizens are together "in the same boat," in that we must all live in the society we create through our personal projections, and our tolerances for abuse, corruption and injustice. This is why the solution to nearly every problem in the world comes down to greater awareness, compassion, and empathy. The roots of all commonwealth are planted in the understanding that we are all the same human beings. What we do to others, we do to ourselves.

If you are a police officer who is being ordered, or peer pressured to carry out indecent and immoral acts, you must break the ranks of that thin blue line, and subdue or even arrest fellow officers who are abusing their office. The *voice of reason* within you is the leadership the world needs. If you stand by idly, and watch your fellow officers and commanders commit injustices, then you become an accomplice to those injustices. Never feel fearful, ashamed or embarrassed to stand up and do what is right.

Following your *voice of reason* may cause you to be ridiculed or even temporarily branded a traitor by your superiors and peers. Even the public may not recognize or appreciate your heroic actions, but even if you are persecuted, ridiculed or ignored, you must speak out against wrongdoing. The lone, ordinary person, existing incognito within the system has tremendous power in a revolution. The silent heroic traitor is always the master source of new eras of progress. The world is always waiting for courageous leadership to advance human excellence and achievement.

At all times, and especially during times of social change and protest, the public and police need to be as sensitive to one another as possible. We are all part of this global community and need to cooperate in order to bring about a safe and secure environment, for all of us to enjoy the beautiful opportunities of life. But there are no shortcuts or quick fixes to these problems. The prisons are full of society's "quick fixes"; they are brimming with our failures as a community of responsibility. It is in the prisons that we hide away our shame and thoughtless creations as a society. Shortcuts will never work. The path to healing and health involves deep and honest introspection and a resolute, clear intention to challenge our antiquated mindsets, and evolve into the heart-space of greater compassion, love and understanding. Progress and healing involves seeing every person as not so different from ourselves. This is the absolute truth.

The ultimate solution is revealed by understanding and honoring what is real. The office of citizen and the office of police are just temporary creations of choice. We made it all up. They are temporary. Look at the many constructs which are born as projected thought-forms, like the three-letter agencies we see come-and-go based on the supposed need of the times. Place your allegiance and respect in what is everlasting and real, not in the transitory and false. People are real. Feelings, emotions, pain and suffering are real. The elements, minerals and environment are real. The plants and animals are real. Human beings—human beings just like you, are real. Please, honor what is real. Please, protect what is real.

The Right to Evolution through Reform or Revolution

"I became convinced that noncooperation with evil is as much a moral obligation as is cooperation with good. No other person has been more eloquent and passionate in getting this idea across than Henry David Thoreau. As a result of his writings and personal witness, we are the heirs of a legacy of creative protest."

—**Martin Luther King, Jr.**

It is your right to protest and be a component of social evolution and revolution, just as it is your right to breathe. There is no hurtful or violent spirit in true revolution, for if that dark spirit is present, then it is not true revolution, but is even a step backwards. You do not build an oracle of enlightenment and freedom on a foundation of brutality. True revolution advances consciousness. Revolution that does not advance us toward higher consciousness and compassion is devolution. For the spirit of revolution is rooted in the principle that eventually there will be an accounting for past injustices, and a reform in the state of consciousness that allowed them to occur. Those involved in revolution would be wise to heed what this implies. Revolution is simple. It is like breathing—out with the old, and in with the new. One thing revolution is not is timid, submissive or obedient. Revolution is defiant.

On the other hand, the nature of oppression can be very tame, and often goes by the false name of civility. It is with a cold and inhumane civility that many great crimes are carried out against the warm hearts of good people. Inside of every good person there is also something very wild. Freedom is wild, and to be free we must at times live dangerously and wildly. We must at times deny the false world its identity, and reject its so-called civil order, and be fearless. There is no prison that can hold a free mind. Divest yourself from the machinery of society's most cruel values, and rebuild them with love. Submission to the unnatural forces of societal coercion is a voluntary process; you can rescind your voluntary submission with a single thought. Your soul exists outside of the jurisdiction of any entity. Give no earthly master permission to subdue your unique truth.

There is something greater than any nation; it is the spirit which created the nation. As a citizen of any country you have a natural allegiance to something deeper than your citizenship. There is a deeply obscured level beyond citizen— it is the domain that gave birth to the space for the constructs of citizen and country to exist. This is your true domain as a free creator and it is to this space your highest gratitude, loyalty and belonging should ascend. Upon this earth we have no obligation whatsoever to uphold any institution, country or idea that does not serve as a humble refuge for all of humanities tender frailties. When people of any country begin to capitalize on their weakest members and even their sick and dying, then their national dream is dead already, and has become a nightmare. Let us revolt against the nightmare, and work together for a kinder world. Non-violence is the highest master tool, example and way, but way for what? It is the way of creating the dream we all know is the ultimate truth.

It is not necessary to dignify tyranny with anger, which merely validates its false power. The ultimate defiance is to simply and gently be your own truth. The ultimate defiance is to simply BE. The ultimate protest is to simply do what is right and good. Lay down your worldly attachments and merely exist in total cooperation with your own unique inner truth. A person who wants nothing fears nothing. Your power is total and unstoppable. There is no single power on earth, nor any person, nor any institution, which has access to ANY power source beyond what you have direct access to right now, in this very moment. We are all fueled by the same free source of life and liberty.

Creativity is the greatest expression of liberty. Understand your power. Live dangerously. Live truthfully. Live freely. Live fearlessly. Cower before no earthly master. Know yourself. Be yourself. Love yourself. Seek goodness and be goodness. Seek beauty and be beauty. Seek love and be love. Once you realize what you really are, you cannot be stopped. The nightmare spirit of control has always been, and is, profoundly stupid. Historically we can see that any attempt to control has always fueled the heart of revolution. We are in power because we control the resources, because we are the resources. People are the resource—the human resource. All natural, organic human-resource currencies are presently difficult for us to recognize, because they are obscured by the petrodollar economies. Absent our uncontrollable petrol addiction and the unsustainable, cancerous growth it causes, it would be easier to see the obviousness that we are a community and family of humans, and we are all in this together. Together we have the resources to sustain one another. People are the final answer to the real call for freedom. The dreamer's untamed eye sees beyond the illusions to the heart of what is real. All power constructs are thought-forms of consensus reality that only exist because we choose to support them collectively with the human resources of the human heart, mind and hand. We possess control of the ultimate resource—US. You will never be a better citizen than when you are dreaming, creating, challenging, discussing, protesting and adding your voice to the great, considerate and humble discussion, presently called —democracy.

Protest is an effective path to change. We have a responsibility to disobey and violate unjust rules and laws. Civil disobedience is a wonderful tool that has shown itself to be one of the most effective and powerful vehicles to speedy social evolution. Non-violent, but absolutely defiant non-cooperation through acts of public civil disobedience are powerful and nearly uncontrollable tools of social reform. They are tools which throw a wrench into the government's obtuse machinery, forcing even the most blind of organizations to crack open their eyes for a moment of self-reflection. This is of course because the survival of the political organism is being threatened through challenges to its identity, the identity being primarily that of control. To challenge that identity results in a loss of power and relevancy, by preventing the organism from being able to exercise its core competency of control.

We must always speak our truth. If one cannot speak their truth, and be their own truth, then what is life beyond an unbearable lie? Any construct that prevents our creative voice from spontaneously flowing and adding richness to our world must be eliminated. Sometimes that expression of richness seeks to reach out and neutralize injustice and tyranny. Peace is not passive. Peace is, at times, a verb that expands in all directions, like a great circle of defiant love reaching for every destination at once. Peace adores above everything free discussion and expression without intimidation. How can we be free to express ourselves, if others are not free to do the same? The master key of real personal truth is that others should be able to live by their truth. It is one of our primary duties to speak up and protest against those who would force or trick us to live by their lies. You can know something is a lie when it has no love in it.

Peter Finch as Howard Beale in the 1976 movie, *Network*, galvanized a country by articulating a popular rage, and by encouraging people to come out of their homes and apartments and communicate. His suggestion was we can fix the problems once we get the conversation going.

> I don't have to tell you things are bad. Everybody knows things are bad. It's a depression. Everybody's

out of work or scared of losing their job. The dollar buys a nickel's worth. Banks are going bust. Shopkeepers keep a gun under the counter. Punks are running wild in the street and there's no one anywhere that seems to know what to do with us. Now into it. We know the air is unfit to breathe, our food is unfit to eat, and we sit watching our TVs while some local newscaster tells us that today we had 15 homicides and 63 violent crimes as if that's the way it's supposed to be. We know things are bad. Worse than bad. They're crazy. It's like everything everywhere is going crazy so we don't go out anymore. We sit in a house as slowly the world we're living in is getting smaller and all we say is, "Please, at least leave us alone in our living rooms. Let me have my toaster, and TV, and my steel belted radials and I won't say anything." Well I'm not going to leave you alone. I want you to get mad. I don't want you to protest. I don't want you to riot. I don't want you to write to your congressman because I wouldn't know what to tell you to write. I don't know what to do about the depression and the inflation and the Russians and the crying in the streets. All I know is first you've got to get mad. You've got to say, "I'm a human being. God Dammit, my life has value." So, I want you to get up now. I want all of you to get up out of your chairs. I want you to get up right now and go to the window, open it, and stick your head out, and yell, "I'm as mad as hell, and I'm not going to take this anymore!" I want you to get up right now. Get up. Go to your windows, open your windows, and stick your head out, and yell, "I'm as mad as hell and I'm not going to take this anymore!" Things have got to change my friends. You've got to get mad. You've got to say, "I'm as mad as hell and I'm not going to take this anymore!" Then we'll figure out what to do about the depression and the inflation and the oil crisis. But first get up out of your chairs, open your window, stick your head out and yell, "I'm as mad as hell and I'm not going to take this anymore!"

One of the most powerful ways of speaking up and expressing our truth is through the means of non-violent protests. Protesting is never a disturbance of the peace. Corruption, injustice, war and intimidation are disturbances of the peace; protesting is merely a response to those disturbances. Freedom of assembly, which can be used as in protest, is in theory protected by the First Amendment of the United States Constitution and is part of the Bill of Rights. It states, "Congress shall make no law respecting an establishment of religion, or prohibiting the free exercise thereof; or abridging the freedom of speech, or of the press; or the right of the people peaceably to assemble, and to petition the Government for a redress of grievances." This suggests that as long as our protests are peaceable, we are free to assemble and allow the *voice of reason* within us each to join others in a conversation. Unfortunately the realities on the street are often very different from promised rights—no matter the country. Too often our conversations through protest are cut short by rude interruptions from the agents of concentrated power, which do not want to hear what change has to say. But change is inevitable and unstoppable. Life moves forward, not backward, and it would be wise to listen to what change has to say. Change may knock lightly on the door of antiquated thinking at first, but when the old mindsets bolt the door, change may rip it from the frame. Change has no master, no limitations and no fear. Change has no ideology, no dogma and no rationality. Change, like time, will wait until the graveyards are full of old ideas. Change can be beautiful, when we are brave enough to evolve with it, and change can be brutal, when we fearfully resist.

An important part of revolution is thinking for oneself and diversifying sources of information and education. Defiance and creativity go hand-in-hand. As Martin Luther King, Jr. said over and over, the world is in dire need of an *"International Association for the Advancement of Creative Maladjustment."* Much of education today focuses on obedience skills rather than critical thinking skills. This is because if you teach a child true critical thinking skills, you potentially create a problem for the system, because the system is profoundly nonsensical, and the child is likely to challenge or reject the system. Young adult students possessing true critical thinking skills are unmanageable, and therefore undesirable to many schools.

Too many people have been cut off from their own self-knowledge and critical thinking abilities. They are cocooned by the comfort of assumptions in a type of developmental stasis. They exist in an obedient, placated "status quo" or autopilot mode of existence. Their growth is stymied, effectively encasing their untapped and unique brilliance in a psychological tumor. Such is the bigot, the misogynist, the xenophobe, the common corporate drone, the academic elitist, the housewife vacuuming her way to heaven, the zealot nationalist whose extreme patriotism includes a feeling of superiority over other countries, and the modern-day vapid college graduate, who has only been readied for obedient submission to a life of mediocrity and corporate servitude.

There can be no revolution without an overthrow of the institutions of education. Centralized authority in education, which is simply a hierarchical, state-controlled institution of government imposed homogenization and "equality," is simply another form of social oppression, where unique individualism is being replaced with institutionalized faux "excellence." It is yet another example of how social monocultures suppress the wild growth that is possible in the untamed forest of innovation without limits. We should guide education away from its commercial, corporate, consumerist orientation, and toward a goal of helping individuals attain inner maturity, balance and a deeply rewarding sense of fulfillment. We should support and foster building organic relationships among all educational disciplines. This would allow each person to develop their own unique calling in society through a wider spectrum of experiences.

When education is decentralized and set free, there is more room for less restrictive apprenticeships and mentoring. Because of the diversity of learning opportunities—a more accommodating system of peer-review and validation can exist. We need to be more open minded about education, and especially there needs to be more acceptance of critical thinking, including toward the system itself. What is the current path and platform for auto-didactics, revolutionaries, trendsetters, misfits, rebels, innovators, people who ask why, alternative thinkers, radical reformers, cultural icons, mould-breakers, geniuses and critical thinkers? Real education is about revolution.

Does society drive revolutionaries underground into isolation, or openly celebrate their uniqueness? The answer appears to be both. The word *celebrity* comes from our *celebration* of those who conquer fear and dare to be different. Originality is coveted by society, yet it is also subject to society's judgment, fear and impulse to identify and pick-at things that are different. From an early age children quickly and naturally identify and pay attention to what is different. This tendency can also be observed in nature, when an animal with odd markings, features or behaviors is killed or rejected by the other members of its species, pack or clan. This is why leading-edge people and sometimes so-called celebrities are the subject of both criticism and adoration. We all know it takes courage to put yourself out there, and we respect people who take that bold and sometimes dangerous risk for us, when perhaps our social fears keep us frozen in our place. Those fears and concerns are legitimate, because being different sometimes comes with real risks. But difference is worth the risk, and may even be a coveted characteristic because those genetic, mental or social aberrations could actually lead to entirely new species, knowledge disciplines or social structures that make the subject of that variation stronger. But at the same time the unknown is feared and what is new is certainly unknown. Yet, real education must be about discovering the unknown, and whenever education becomes a system of conformity it is no longer useful.

In 1998, Apple, Inc. won an *Emmy Award* for Best Commercial, and also won the 2000 *Grand Effie Award* for their ad campaign which—no matter its corporate source— deeply resonated with the respect we all have for those who dare to think and act differently:

> Here's to the crazy ones. The misfits. The rebels. The troublemakers. The round pegs in the square holes. The ones who see things differently. They're not fond of rules. And they have no respect for the status quo. You can quote them, disagree with them, glorify or vilify them. About the only thing you can't do is ignore them. Because they change things. They push the human race forward. While some may see them as the crazy ones, we see genius. Because the people who are crazy enough to think they can change the world, are the ones who do.

Rebellious and adventurous souls have a way of leading us off the edge of the map, where the dragons are, to confront those dark beasts of our fear and ignorance. The spirit of discovery cannot be cultivated on an assembly line of desks in classrooms. We must question the seats of authority, especially in education, and seek to understand what "valid" is and where authority originates. By breaking down the monocultures in education and building individualized community learning networks for all ages, we can go beyond the bureaucratic limitations of graded classrooms, standardized curricula, reductionist testing and mandatory attendance in isolated buildings called "schools."

Certainly not all schools and universities are "bad," and many are wonderful, but they are <u>not</u> the only sources of legitimate learning which should be recognized. Many of today's universities are run like diploma mills, turning out tens of thousands of students who paid huge sums of money for their piece of paper, and who are entirely unprepared to meet life's real challenges, and most importantly, to meet them with vigor and brilliance as original contributors to human knowledge and wisdom. Much of the educational system is a broken relic, a symbol of shortsightedness and corporate greed. The Department of Education and the accreditation agencies have become monopolistic bureaucracies that have killed the diversity in education. Real freedom does not need permission to teach or to learn. In a free society a full spectrum of education providers are free to meet the diverse needs of its learners. The adage buyer beware is the test of any assertion of value. It is incumbent upon all literate and free people to investigate and evaluate the worth and validity of any educational institution's assertion of value upon its students, faculty and programs. Licensing and accreditation monopolies arguably harm education more than they help. But knowledge truly is power. Real knowledge and truth cannot be invalidated. Knowledge changes things, even if that knowledge does not have a seal of approval from the power structures. This concept is revolution in action. Real education is valuable, no matter where it comes from: an ivy league school, a public library or your grandmother. Real education needs no official validation, it is validated by its usefulness and integrity, which are currencies universally accepted.

No one owns exclusive control of free minds, mutual consent of association, words, ideas, creativity, philosophies, beliefs or opinions. The revolution of real education is in understanding that education is about ideas! You cannot regulate or control an idea. Ideas do not submit to, or acknowledge any jurisdiction other than the jurisdictions of creativity and the mutual consent of peers. This is why revolution happens, because ideas have a life of their own, and the new generations eventually supplant the old ideas with their own. Young people do not need a "traditional" education, they ARE the education. The young will teach the old the new ways, and the old will adapt or perish. The essential lesson the student needs to know is they do not need anything because the path to their future is already written into the fabric of their being. As you blossom, your sweet gift is the literal future of society through the unique imprint of your innovations, ideas and contributions. The crumbling establishment needs fertile young minds more than young people need the establishment. When you ask "why," and defy the system, and poke at what seems broken, you become the revolution by spurring the transformation from what is—into what will be.

Apple's CEO, Steve Jobs, who ordered the creation of the previously mentioned *Think Different* campaign, said in an interview for the 1994 PBS documentary, *One Last Thing*:

> When you grow up you tend to get told the world is the way it is and your life is just to live your life

inside the world. Try not to bash into the walls too much. Try to have a nice family life, have fun, save a little money. That's a very limited life. Life can be much broader once you discover one simple fact, and that is—everything around you that you call life was made up by people that were no smarter than you. And you can change it, you can influence it, you can build your own things that other people can use. The minute that you understand that you can poke life and actually something will, you know if you push in, something will pop out the other side, that you can change it, you can mold it. That's maybe the most important thing. It's to shake off this erroneous notion that life is there and you're just gonna live in it, versus embrace it, change it, improve it, make your mark upon it. I think that's very important and however you learn that, once you learn it, you'll want to change life and make it better, cause it's kind of messed up, in a lot of ways. Once you learn that, you'll never be the same again.

Real education creates revolutionaries rather than suppressing them. At the very heart of every revolution is the free flow of information. Lifelong learning is like a never ending personal revolution. Why not make that revolution of enlightenment available to everyone at all times? We should open the floodgates of availability to open and free learning for all people. Any community would benefit from having more literate, critical thinkers among its population. When knowledge becomes a profit center, guards and bars must be placed around the vault of wisdom, and educators and administrators become knowledge profiteers in the war against ignorance. They become information bankers, holding knowledge ransom for a fee, which is a self-destructive enterprise to any forward-seeking society.

The truly astute master teacher has learned the lesson of humility. True education seeks to set its students free, not to hold them captive to antiquated standards, or to ensnare them in debt. The student always becomes the master, and such is the revolutionary transition of power between generations. Young people are the future, and we must believe in them. Anyone who resists revolution or pooh-poohs an emerging revolution is grossly ignorant of the fact that life without evolution is extinction. And while every revolution may not be forward moving, all forward movement is revolutionary. We must therefore at least give serious consideration to the messages of those on the front lines of change. The supreme lesson of any education should be to think for yourself and to be yourself; absent this attainment, education creates dangerous, stupefying conformity.

While change of revolution can be wonderful, the perturbations of change can involve disturbances and threats to safety. Just because someone is fighting for something they passionately believe in, does not mean they are impervious to harm. There are many obstacles you may face and some can be extremely dangerous. It is of paramount importance that you comport yourself with peaceful conduct and respectful calm. For example, never engage the police directly in the realm of their expertise. The jurisdiction of the system and its agents and officers is control, force and violence. This is where they train, drill and exist at all times. You do not want to engage them in the jurisdiction of their expert training, for once you are on the turf of their highest capability, your normal rights are effectively suspended, and you may be hurt or even killed. When engaging the system and its officers and agents, you must conduct yourself with wisdom and intelligence.

It is also very important to be aware of, and avoid being party to igniting a chain reaction of the mob mentality, which has a life-force of its own as a collective behavioral entity. Mob mentality is a form of situational "groupthink" that can cause people in large groups to potentially engage in abnormally negative activities. For example, if one protester in a crowd picks up a rock and throws it at a police officer, then other members in the same group may begin to do the same. Protests should not lead to mob frenzies, where upset and angry people are just reacting to and amplifying destructive base impulses. There may be a legitimate cause for people to be angry and upset, but we must deeply strive to remain in an elevated state of mind. This can be accomplished by meditating on and possessing a strong understanding of what the protest is trying to achieve. During a protest keep in the forefront of your thoughts a mindfulness of the sacred space that condemns suppression, in all of its forms, and protects and promulgates any thoughts, words and actions that produce holistic healing for all. This holistic and compassionate mindset is very different from the mindset of retaliation through violent force, threats or wild and incendiary mob insanity. Before beginning any kind of collective gathering, each individual should make sure they are in a sound mindset, and are committed and able to carry out their protest through non-violent means. All it takes is the spark of one person to ignite a raging fire. You are going to want to practice what you preach and be the change that proves justice can be protected and preserved without the use of violence and force. Be that proof of great possibility. After all, if you are protesting against suppression, control and violence, and succumbing to those base compulsions in the process, you will diminish your moral stance, and you could be harmed, or cause the unintended harm of others.

All people learn from example by watching others, especially their role models. People learn from example more than they learn from instruction. This is why "do as I say, and not as I do" has very little respectability as a teaching philosophy. We create in people through our actions and example. In this way people around us become reflections of our own behavioral patterns and internal energies.

When trying to teach someone a boundary, they learn less from the enforcement of the boundary and more from the way the boundary is established. To teach a person to be calm, one must teach the lesson <u>with</u> calm—not aggression. To teach a person to be reasonable, one must teach <u>with</u> reason—not force. One of the most powerful teaching tools is listening, because all people yearn for acceptance and everyone wants to be heard.

Teaching the system a lesson is the same way. As an activist, your message means less than the way the message is delivered, because in actuality, the way the message is delivered, IS the message. This is why non-violence is the way. Only non-violent methods can teach the lesson of non-violence. While it is true that large-scale social change requires many individuals working together, change still begins with each individual. This is why Mohandas Gandhi's implied message that each person must "be the change we wish to see in the world" is among the most sage and eternally wise concepts ever put forth, and represents one of the core lessons Dr. Arun Gandhi learned from his grandfather. The famous "be the change" message is a common paraphrase, which succinctly attempts to capture the essence of the following text from, *The Collected Works of M.K.Gandhi*:

> We but mirror the world. All the tendencies present in the outer world are to be found in the world of our body. If we could change ourselves, the tendencies in the world would also change. As a man changes his own nature, so does the attitude of the world change towards him. This is the divine mystery supreme. A wonderful thing it is and the source of our happiness.

There are many effective ways to confront power, as every dragon has a missing scale of vulnerability and weakness. The system does not understand love or kindness, only rules. Love bewilders, discombobulates and unbalances the rigid stance of all agencies of foul and unjust power. Publicity and transparency scatter the strong, powerful agents of control into the shadows. Like all cowards, brutes in any number flee when their spell of fear has no effect. Fear has no effect on love. Even monsters will protect something beautiful, because it reminds them of a small part within themselves they wish was larger. Being love-filled and beautiful is almost unconquerable. Love absorbs the hard blows of rigid fists; love surrounds, softens and tires violence and force. If you are confronted, bullied or intimidated, while expressing your *voice of reason*, remember this protective strategy—be beautiful. Being love-filled and beautiful is one of the most powerful defenses that one can employ. Imagine that you are a beautiful and unique flower growing in life's garden. Most people will not intentionally step on a beautiful flower. If you are walking through the garden and you see the beautiful flowers, you will walk around them to avoid destroying their delicate beauty. Even most "mean people" and "bad people," otherwise known as people in pain and crisis, try to avoid the destruction of beauty by their own hand. They recognize beauty and secretly wish more of their own beauty was dominant. And even when the rare soul who enjoys trampling and crushing the beautiful flowers comes along, they quickly discover that there are many gardeners who tend life's garden, and these gardeners do not like people stepping on the beautiful flowers. You do not have to do anything to defend yourself in life; just BE beautiful, and life will defend you. The most effective activism is kindness. Be beautiful and you are doing your part to create a more beautiful world.

Free Expression as the Master Catalyst of Change

"The peculiar evil of silencing the expression of an opinion is, that it is robbing the human race; posterity as well as the existing generation; those who dissent from the opinion, still more than those who hold it. If the opinion is right, they are deprived of the opportunity of exchanging error for truth; if wrong, they lose, what is almost as great a benefit, the clearer perception and livelier impression of truth, produced by its collision with error."

—John Stuart Mill, On Liberty, 1859

There is seldom a clear, structured solution to complex problems; there never will be, and to believe so is extreme hubris. So do not listen to critics who proclaim that your positions or protests are without merit unless they are accompanied by a clear solution. It is also unnecessary that everyone be of the same opinion, so do not listen to critics who say your opinions are invalid because they are inconsistent. Systemic problems have systemic solutions, and the right ideas will emerge through the process of dialogue.

This is how ideas work, and open-minded critical thinkers should always be willing to engage in dialogue, despite any differences of opinion.

Consider each mind as a flower, which goes through its own cycles of growth, budding, bloom and decay. Somewhere along the path, the cerebral flower of the mind comes into full bloom, and through dialogue with others and cross-communication begins a wondrous process of cross-pollination with other mind-flowers. Before you know it, new flowers with new colors, patterns and shapes begin to emerge everywhere; idea-flowers which have never existed before, not even in our wildest imagination. This process exposes the genius of natural designs and laws which are far beyond our weak intellect's comprehension. What is essential is that we come together in community and communicate, and do so as respectfully as possible. The change will emerge on its own, and will carry the unique imprints of each participant forward into the mysterious creation of that which is beyond imagination—a new world.

True evolution is beyond the myopic sight of political thought-forms, or empty clamor and rebellion. True evolution is a journey into the vast gateway of new vocabularies, concepts and even expanded understandings of life itself. It is about taking those new vocabularies, which often belong to new generations, and speaking new languages, and through those languages, creating new narratives; narratives that could have never been expressed without those many new constructs. We may encounter resistance and find new understandings to be a source of fear and confusion, yet as human creatures we are nonetheless deeply compelled to evolve, and this is an inexorable and natural process.

The process of social evolution is a natural emergence, based on the community of social interaction and communications. This underscores one of the reasons why freedom of expression and freedom of peaceable assembly must remain sacrosanct. This especially true of dissenting opinions and acts of absolute opposition and defiance against injustice. It is everyone's duty to oppose all forms of injustice, particularly the act of trying to silence the exchanging of ideas in relevant venues where dialogue is needed. The higher mind universally condemns any use of force, which seeks to intimidate, impede or squelch free expression and peaceful assembly by those wishing to enter into the conversation of change.

It is hardly possible to conceive of any act more disturbing than the intimidation of another free person. It is unimaginable that any person or opposition group, including government or police, would dare to touch another person's body; dare to lay a hand upon a free, human being. It is unconscionable! We must always stand in solidarity and in absolute defiance against such acts. Unless you are harming someone, you should never be touched.

Never stand by and allow a hand of intimidation to be placed upon the sacred and free body of an unwilling participant, nor allow a monster to reach into the mind or heart, and silence a free soul, with fear and threat of liberty lost. The most cunning enemy comes at your energy, image or name, but the base and ignorant brute, the foul pig of a despot launches his whole selfish being—mind and body upon you, to suffocate your freedom.

No law should allow or promote the silencing of opinions, or the directing or disbanding of peaceable assembly. Strangled in the clutch of brute intimidation, we are all made victims; first by the foul deed, and second by those good souls who do nothing to oppose it. Any law, or law body enabling such injustice, must be reformed, and must be relentlessly ignored, with loving contempt.

Humanity is full of beautiful people; unique and precious, each of us are fine, worthy and wondrous beings. Every person has something meaningful to say in the conversation of life. Let people speak. Let people disagree. Communicate. Listen. Have high-respect, if not for your opponent, then for your own comportment and conduct as a good listener. Don't make the mistake of thinking that you have to agree with people and their beliefs to defend them from injustice. As free as you allow others to be, such freedom you create for yourself. We each have a miraculous capacity within our mind to evolve and to learn new ways of understanding. The great procession of life's challenges and conflicts ever advance, and every difficult moment is a new opportunity for each of us to showcase the evolved state of humanity we all wish to see.

When you close your eyes to what apparently "is," and look inward to the infinite truth of what is possible through imagination, you will discover vast landscapes of uncharted territory, clear open spaces for all people to exist together in harmony. We can build these beautiful visions together, through respect. The essential respect is the one in your own heart for yourself. The expansion of your own consciousness, capacity for love, humility and compassion—this is the path; this is the way.

A Self Revolution through Love, Intention and Service

"TO BE HOPEFUL in bad times is not just foolishly romantic. It is based on the fact that human history is a history not only of cruelty, but also of compassion, sacrifice, courage, kindness. What we choose to emphasize in this complex history will determine our lives. If we see only the worst, it destroys our capacity to do something. If we remember those times and places—and there are so many— where people have behaved magnificently, this gives us the energy to act, and at least the possibility of sending this spinning top of a world in a different direction. And if we do act, in however small a way, we don't have to wait for some grand utopian future. The future is an infinite succession of presents, and to live now as we think human beings should live, in defiance of all that is bad around us, is itself a marvelous victory."

—**Howard Zinn**

Some people have pointed to a combination of ignorance, groupthink and irrationality as the root issues causing humanity's problems, and believe more rational and logical thinking will save us. The Latin roots of animus reveal insight into the model of the rational mind as our savior. It seems that the strong guiding hands of the intellect and logic of "Big Daddy" must save us once again. But in the roots of animus, along with "the mind," "intellect" and "rational soul in man," we also encounter the animus of hostile dislike and enmity of the displeased—"Big Daddy," an avatar of animosity, vehemence and wrath, and the source of piercing logical intellect. Maybe this is part of the reason we seem to worship intelligence. But we have all seen the cold, calculating intellect and its sometimes reptilian, sterile precision. We have all witnessed the battles between feelings and facts, logic and love, and intellect and emotion. We have all noted masculine and feminine styles of command and control, versus communication and cooperation. Yet, for some reason we always turn to the animus, the rational soul in man, for the answers, and we say, "if our rational mind and intelligence cannot save us, what can?"

Rationality alone cannot save us, and believing it can is just another mind trap. We will never "think" our way out of our troubles. We are not rational, logical beings, and never will be. We are like cells in a large organism, and we receive and process messages in the same way which is observable in cellular biology. Each cell in the body is being bombarded with thousands of messages at once, from other cells near and far, instructing the cell to divide, not divide or to commit suicide (apoptosis). Similarly, we are also continuously receiving messages from other people through the media, and through our community and families, and we must intuitively synthesize all of this ambient information in order to make personal decisions. How does a couple decide to have a child? They read many messages from the economy and world politics, to their local family and community support, and innumerable other variables. This is very similar to a cell deciding to divide. This colloidal, dynamic and intuitive communication process is complex to the point of being almost magical. We have always used the term "magic" to describe any phenomenon that the intellect can not explain. That is why the individual process of decision making may seem like magic, since it involves all perceptive parts of our total being and is much more than the narrow, so called rational and logical process.

The lesson to be learned here is to listen to yourself. Where do you get your messages from, your own inner-guide and *voice of reason*, or Madison Avenue? Is your original voice even yours, or was it branded into your soul through commercials between cartoons? Who are you, really? We must stop allowing propagandists to manipulate our emotions; the steering wheel of our total being. As an organism, your inner-intelligence knows how to keep you safe. As a being of mysterious complexity, listening to the essence of natural messengers will lead you in the right direction, but you must squelch out any external noise, if you wish to hear the sublime *voice of reason* within.

Do not think of this as "spiritual" if you have a problem with that thought-form or term; just recognize these complex communications as something beyond our complete understanding, beyond science, and beyond full description.

We can call it natural or nature (deeply connected to nurture), or we can simply call it being. How many times have you wished you would have listened to your intuition and inner voice? Do not let words, logic and reason get in the way of your reliance upon this amazing inner awareness. There is enormous power and wisdom in intuition and simple, natural beingness.

The intuitive spirit-nature we all possess is a beautiful gift, but too often that gift is suppressed. In many ways people have been denatured and lost that magnificent gift. In the physical realm, the best athletes do not rely solely on knowing all the different technical aspects of their game. While technical knowledge is useful, it is only a small part of a true master's brilliance. The master of any craft is first a master of self, cooperating with innate intelligence within. They detach themselves from the rote instructions and trust in instincts to emerge naturally to carry them forward to excellence. That is why you cannot create a champion athlete. All you can do is free the person to access their own innate potential.

Knowledge works the same way. We already have everything that we need to know in our intuition and our instincts. It is pointless trying to absorb all the knowledge in the world. That is partly because we do not need so much of it, and partly because we can never achieve knowing everything in our lifetime. What we do need is to be open to what we already have within us.

Knowledge can be useful as a tool and reference point, but only as a beginning of a greater journey to something so much bigger, and yet so much more simple and liberating. People who seek after knowledge for knowledge's sake become trapped in a process where the means becomes the end. That is so sad. They are like a crippled Beethoven forever learning how to compose, instead of simply writing down the beautiful music that is written into the fabric of their souls already. People like that become seekers for seeking's sake, and they seldom experience the joy of knowledge as a state of consciousness. Instead, they spend their lives trying to learn everything that exists beyond them, in the hope of finding the truth that already lies within.

This is the battle between the cunning human mind and the quiet, intuitive inner-self. Connecting with essential truth and knowing oneself is the only way. Surrender is the path to freedom through our unique authenticity, where we experience the flow of life not through the narrow lens of the mind, but through the vast refuge of the heart. As Joseph Campbell said, "follow your bliss." This concept speaks to the ultimate path as humility and surrender. Nothing else is needed. Freedom is the realization that it is sufficient to simply be a human being. The answer is balance. The answer is intelligent compassion. The answer is love. It is the self-revolution of greater individual consciousness that is the absolute path to humanity's next great step forward. All revolution begins with self. How can you create something pure, when you are yourself an unnatural creation? True creation requires authority and authenticity. When you are not free, you are not creating; you are being created. If you are a creation of conditioning, then part of your new creations really comes from what created you. So, in this sense, revolution is really about a personal revolution of consciousness first.

If you want to be successful at anything you do, it will help you to first be a successful human. Since human life is a social life, becoming a successful human means being there for other people. No time is better spent than that spent in the service of your fellow man. We are here to spend ourselves on others; for each person is a great treasure. Success does not just mean happiness, success means doing the right thing—and this ultimately leads to happiness. The rewards of doing the right thing are usually much deeper and painful. The greatest happiness comes from feeling and expressing our love for other people, and particularly our families. If you think about it, we love most those who we serve most, whether it be children, employees, friends or our communities. And this means that we can bring about a greater love for one another, though a life of simple, but meaningful service.

There is a great indelible interconnectedness of humanity. When we fail our friends and neighbors, and even the stranger down the way, through our vanity, selfishness, greed, envy, fear, indifference, or complacency, something dies in us all. When we fail to even know about, or acknowledge someone's suffering, which is in obvious sight, much less attempt to ease it, the world is made a darker place. The failure of that individual to act represents an atomic failure of humanity itself. The world markets of optimism and hope can plummet because of the actions or inactions of a single person. The upside to this is that the good works of even one person can represent the whole of humanity's triumph through that sole heroic act. In reality, one person can make a difference, and a difference that can move through the masses as a seismic wave, transforming an entire ethos overnight. Look at the enormous impact the frail-bodied Gandhi had on two violently clashing countries with his simple spiritual exercises of defiance, selflessness, loving other people and valuing human life. And that was even without the power of media to move his ideas around quickly. Like a cultural or emotional butterfly effect, one person really can make a difference. Each person is the revolution.

There are many types of currency, not the least of which is a system of emotional and trust economics that govern societies, both primitive and modern. These economics govern every relationship, whether it be between individuals or nations. In fact, money as we know it does not really exist. Money is a thought-form. Money is just a piece of paper, and outside of our dynamic and collective consent it has no value beyond the value of the paper it is printed on. The only reason money has value is because we all agree that it does. So, ironically, money could be seen as a placeholder for trust. We trust that when we go to redeem that worthless piece of paper (or its digital representation in an account) the recipient will honor its value with real-world goods and services at a fair exchange. In a relationship, when trust is lost, everything is lost. We are all in a relationship with one another. We can become emotionally bankrupt, or even in debt. And this is why it is important that we invest in people with our personal currency of service, restoring those whose personal accounts of hope and optimism are low.

There are so many people in need, who are quietly hovering near the abysmal edges of emotional bankruptcy. Life is dynamic, and it can be ugly. Thomas Hobbes wrote in *Leviathan* that life was, "solitary, poor, nasty, brutish, and short." And Henry David Thoreau wrote in *Walden* that, "The mass of men lead lives of quiet desperation." Too many people are living those lives of quiet desperation. This is one of the reasons so many people anesthetize themselves with a never-ending, gluttonous consumption of mass entertainment, television, technology and fruitless consumerism. The rise of technology, corporatism and consumerism has slowly smothered out a way of relating to the world that seems to be almost lost forever—analogue and in-person. Along with the rise of technology has come a very strange arrogance. There are so many disillusioned and disconnected people out there prancing around because of the powerful technology they use, but what do they really use it for? We have all these shiny, almost magical things, but are we really happier, or wiser? While much of the technology we are senselessly addicted to promises us greater connectedness, people are more isolated, disconnected and lonely, than ever before in history.

People feel more and more insignificant, cut-off and powerless. We are buried in a mountain of information, technology, gadgets, goods and manufactured complexities. We are lost and rendered nearly invisible in a digital snowstorm of super-connectivity. It is a form of anonymity through mass-connection. True community has been nearly eviscerated, and a tactile-less mockery of community has been put in its place. Houses and apartments have become cubical prison-tombs, where millions of screen-irradiated mummies hide from the sunlight, nature, and genuine social interaction. People have social anxiety because of their lack of experience relating to humans in person. At airports and restaurants people eat alone, and strangers seldom talk. Everyone is texting, emailing, rushing, surfing and being connection-entertained with social media, and yet somehow, we are tragically ALONE.

Absent the vital lessons attained through simple face-to-face community interactions, and tainted by the identity propaganda being mass-ejected out of the media weapons for the highest bidders, people soon become observers of life rather than participants. They begin seeing the "good life" as something to attain through goods, services, and external providers, and forget that the so-called *Kingdom of Heaven* is within. It is almost as though people are suffering from dissociative personality disorder, where the constructed consumer-self has no close relationships, except with need providers. Even our life partners can become just another external need provider. Modern consumer life is like a mass dissociative disorder which prevents people from experiencing essential truth, real-life community, universal rites of passage and even an acceptable and reasonable death. Consumer life is essentially a social psychology framework, which seeks to keep your consciousness plugged into their headend of ideals and created needs, for profit. The result of this assault is a growing culture of fear-subdued, disconnected, isolated and mass-distracted people who feel powerless.

Most people do not isolate and anesthetize themselves because they are happily living life; they participate in this self-abuse because they are hiding from life. They are trying to fill an emptiness within. If you are lonely when you are alone, you are in poor company, and many people are poor in the deepest and most internal sense. They will do anything to avoid being left alone with their thoughts, being left alone to Thoreau's quiet desperation, or worn down by the unforgiving and brutish world described by Hobbes. They are teetering on emotional bankruptcy and, though they do not realize it, they are living with the haunting but quiet realization that they are not answering the calls for help from those in need. They have a nagging feeling that they have not yet experienced all of what life has to offer. They want more in their relationships; more money and more success. They try to force these things, and when they do not materialize, they become negative and pessimistic. The harder they try, the further away the things they want seem to move. They do not realize that all success comes through other people. It can seem counterintuitive when you learn that you get most things in life not by taking, but by giving. Giving is the key to all success in all applications of human life. The act of true giving is indistinguishable from receiving. Giving yourself is the ultimate revolution! Giving is not a physical action; giving is a philosophy, and a way of living life. There are endless opportunities to give the smallest things that cost us nothing, but have great value to other people. Money and time are not the only things we can give. We can give others appreciation, patience, compassion, courtesy, kindness, dependability, friendship, forgiveness, gratitude, honesty, loyalty, respect, tolerance and, of course, love.

For example let's look at just one of these—courtesy. Courtesy is a powerful and amazing gift to give. Courtesy is a silver lining around the dark clouds of civilization; it is the best part of refinement and, in many ways, an art of heroic beauty in the vast gallery of man's cruelty and baseness. Good manners are appreciated as much as bad manners are abhorred, and a polite enemy is just as difficult to discredit, as a rude friend is to protect. Mastering courtesy alone will enhance your life and the lives of others. We can give a tired clerk a kind and understanding glance. We can give a frustrated driver a spot in line on the road. We can give a hopeful passerby a kind smile and wave. We can speak to people at all stations of life with respectful and polite words and tones. We can wait with one item in the grocery line behind someone with a full cart with a gentle smile, and body language that makes their day better. When we want to talk, we can instead listen, and let our attentiveness to another's need to speak be our silent statement. All of these simple but powerful gifts have immense value to the person receiving them, and all are examples of an overarching philosophy of giving and service that we can each apply in our lives every day. Simply by thinking about something other than ourselves, and by monitoring our behaviors with a pure and selfless intent of making the lives of other people better, we have the privileged opportunity to change them for the better.

Whether we acknowledge it or not, we all have a debt to the society in which we live. If we want to succeed in society at anything, we must first pay our debt to society. But here is the most important part; our debt never ends. We must pay it each and every day for the rest of our lives. Once you realize this, no matter your philosophical or religious framework, whether it be the golden rule of Christianity, the view of biochemical inducement of self-preservation through the sociological laws of reciprocity, the "Mystical Law" of Karma (the universal law of ethical causation), Confucian Shu reciprocity, good old horse sense of the law of the harvest, or any other world-view construct of the same concept, life will start working for you rather than against you. Life has a way of shining on people who stand in the sunshine of kind actions. But you can't fake it. It has to come from the heart, with a true spirit of giving and selflessness. A talent is no talent, unless it is used for the benefit of other people. Even if you consider your talents a blessing, they may work against you if you do not properly use your precious gifts for the benefit of others. For a moment in this brief existence, we have the privilege to share time with other people, and serve them and their needs. The greatest joys in life are found not only in what we do and feel, but also in our quiet hopes and labors for others. The trees which are pruned, watered and nurtured by caring hands bear the greatest fruits; it is the same with people. It is critical to know that service heals the recipient and the giver. If you have not been served personally by caring hands in your own life, do not be bitter, but instead, ask yourself who you can now serve. If you have had some tough times in life, now more than ever is the time to make someone else's life better. Reject the role of the victim and become the healer and teacher. How we treat other people changes them, but even more so, how we treat other people changes us. This is the wondrous gift of giving; through this act, we receive an important part of our own identity. A person is defined by their actions and intent, and being social creatures, outside of our own useless self-image, the only proof that we exist resides in the minds of other people we change with our actions. So, ask yourself, "How do I change people?" Seek to change people for the better, and and have your existence proved by the raised hands of the people you have served, who will say without doubt that you have cared.

To be of value to us all, these ideas need to be made real in the world. We should speak to protect the ideals of goodness, and act to make them real in the world. The first proves a consummate mind, the second a valorous heart. True progress for humanity is anything that takes us closer to supporting one another. Small acts of kindness between you and the individuals around you are the germination that springs into being something as mysterious as life itself, and what may in fact be humanity's greatest accomplishment— compassion for others. Let us all strive to cultivate a deeper and more meaningful desire to ease the burdens of others. Every person is a precious gift, and we are all like little children who yearn for acceptance, safety, and unconditional love. Let us all reach out with a hope that we could each bring some degree of happiness to other human beings. Let each of us lead a revolution of support in the lives of others.

Many people are now sensing that something important is happening in the world. People are talking, and they "feel" something; they are picking up on something they cannot articulate, but they know it is there. Let's define it before it gets here. Let us enjoin our energy with the good-spirited people around the world in our deepest and most sincere desire to share our own unique gifts, where our greatest achievements are counted as the simple acts that touch, heal and elevate the world for the greater good of all.

Declaring our intentions for a safer and kinder world is the obvious first step toward attaining those goals. Every journey begins with the first step of articulating the intention, and then becoming the intention. We may not be able to change the world overnight, and there is no need for fantasies of creating a utopia, but have faith that we can make some difference in the lives of others. It is possible to advance together, and no matter how slight that advancement is, it will be a resounding triumph for humanity! What would you attempt to do if you knew you could not fail? As Victor Hugo once wrote, "There is one thing stronger than all the armies in the world, and that is an idea whose time has come." The time is each moment called now. Every life is precious. Let us subdue the ravages of the baser-self, and aspire to the higher calling of exalting joy through compassion, for that is the one true purpose of humanity. The change is as simple as changing your mind, and upon that intent the course is set. Start with yourself, and focus on your desires. You cannot change another person's mind or educate them; this they must do themselves. Your own clear intention is what is important. Intention is the foundation of all inner and outer institutions of humanity. It is the basis of legal and judicial systems, all human contracts, and rests at the root of all innovation and progress.

Your intentions define you. People are more than just selfish response to stimuli. Many people have sacrificed themselves to fates that clearly were not based on self-interest by possessing intentions to serve something greater in scope than the self. Thus, deterministic or divine, intention is the seed-germ of all change, and can defy all environments. According to many theologians, the judgment of "the intentions of our hearts" by God, upon our very soul, is predicated upon our innermost intentions. According to philosophers and now even scientists, intention is the foundation of numerous quantum physical and metaphysical universal laws. Intention is the primary concern of all individuals, the collective, the state, and all judgements worldly and purportedly beyond. Prayer, meditation, mantra and affirmation are explicit forms of accessing the power of intention. In short, intention is the only pathway to the future we will likely ever know. We can use this powerful intention.

Many people feel powerless. But one freedom that no influence, power, city, state, government, group, consequence or intimidation can reach to gird, is a free soul's ability to think, and consequently react to the situations of life. The elemental root of our thoughts, the underlying structure upon which our complex ideals and knowledge stands, is our basic intention. Propagandists, research scientists and consumer psychologists work steadily to pry into "black box" of free agency and thought, but thankfully free thought and the indomitable will of the individual have not yet been bridled, or entirely broken, and we still have relatively free minds, if we so choose.

As individuals, it may seem we are not able to control or change the world, but through our willful intentions we may at least escape the culpability of our own complicit minds and hearts. When we oppose oppression, we lift our hands from the collective reins that empower such oppressions. We have the power to oppose, and therefore, not be party to what we see as injustice, even if we belong to a collective that perpetuates the injustice. This is the liberating and defining power of intention.

Through our intentions, a place no power can influence, we have the power to oppose. The terrible atrocities in the world require more from each of us than a regret-filled acknowledgment they exist; they require our most earnest intentions be focused on their immediate eradication. To do this we must first have conscious awareness that it must change. Once our clear intention is set, and we no longer "accept," we will in time begin to see the change the collective will creates. The one and only true freedom we ALL possess is what we think; and our intentions govern what we think.

We all feel that we cannot change the world alone, but as free thinking people we can express our intentions to not live in a world where some humans have, in fact, been reduced to nothing more than mere vessels of pain. We do not have to be victimized by the ugliness in the world any longer. An incubus of ignorance, fear, hunger, oppression and intolerance haunts large regions of the world, and we must have no delusions that we are immune. We must refuse to forget that we too are human, that we too are frail, that we all are subject to such miseries, and in time, we shall all be subject to frailty and suffering.

Acknowledge that everything we have created in the world started as a tiny intention. We carry within us the enormity of possibility that gave birth to everything that has been made in the world. Let us now yearn for the possibility of building a happiness in every heart. Let us now build inward a new world of hope, a world of limitless possibilities for the children of tomorrow, where each soul can reach the heights of their potential to love and to be loved.

We have the power to set our intentions on the betterment of our world. The very "least" among us has the enormous power to effect change through small acts of determination and will. We can each immediately liberate ourselves as victims in the world, through solidifying an intent to act; intent to forgive; intent to love; intent to be caring, polite and empathetic. Then, with that clear intention set into motion through the simplest first actions, we will begin to liberate ourselves from victimization, thereby creating an entirely new perspective and future. It all starts with how you look at the world, and forgiveness and love are integral to the process of healing. There is no love without forgiveness, and there is no forgiveness without love. The conflicts we have with the outside world are often conflicts we have within ourselves. If you do not like a certain behavior in others, look within yourself to find the roots of what discomforts you. Every soul is beautiful and precious; is worthy of dignity and respect, and deserving of peace, joy and love. You will be a beautiful person, as long as you see the beauty in others. This is how you change everything. To have our needs met, to love, to be loved, to feel safe in this world and to each know our purpose, is a simple matter of creating those blessings for others. We have the power to choose these virtues, rather than choosing violence, rage, anger, revenge, greed and other base impulses of the lower-self. We may know our true purpose in life, because we may choose our purpose in life. Our purpose is to be there for one-another. Giving is the master key to success, in all applications of human life.

In each of us exists a gift which has blessed the world with hope time after time. Each person carries within their core the birthright of creative freedom, which, when organized and orchestrated, is the most awesome force on earth. It is a force that can send a human to the moon or send her voice around the world in an instant. It is a power that collectively has always, even after mistakes, re-centered, and inevitably fought for freedom and rights. It is that kernel of promise within each of us which we must harness and responsibly share. You begin by expressing your highest intentions and by declaring your purpose which will be—and is now at this very moment being fulfilled—to rise above any indifference, and irrevocably declare that you too have true, heartfelt compassion and empathy for all who suffer. Through our intentions, we shall stand erect, defiant and without shame, and declare that IT IS POSSIBLE TO MAKE A DIFFERENCE!

The most powerful tools of revolution through intention are humility and consciousness. Humility and full consciousness are inseparable. Once you become fully conscious and self-aware, or awake, you are immediately humble. Only unconscious people, and "sleep-walkers," who do not know themselves and what they really are can lack humility. True humility is greatness. Humility and greatness are not exclusive to one-another, but are fully compatible. Seek to be both great and good, through reclaiming your authenticity. The authentic human has the might of compassion and the creative power to do any manner of good. Humility is not weak. Not being great is a form of extreme arrogance, while being great is an act of true humility. It is arrogant to not be the great and marvelous being you were intended to be. It is supremely neglectful and insulting to the heart of creation to squander your divine birthright. It takes an act of absolute humility to accept the mantle of greatness, which was written into each of our destinies. All strength and greatness comes from humility. We must all be humble enough to be great, and to allow that greatness to carry us through hard times, to better days.

People are in desperate need of your great belief, vision and will. Vast regions of the world are now human slaughter houses, where deserving and once bright and hopeful eyes, now stare blankly toward the last hiding places deep within. Each of these worthy souls have been robbed by poverty, fear and grotesque apathy. They exist as former humans, who should be delightfully moving through the sacrosanct journey of life with dignity, but are instead reduced to mere vessels of pain; they exist each relentless moment as vessels of pure misery.

Cynicism is one of the terrible obstacles to progress. Please lay down your cynicism, and believe in the transformational power of love. Dare to believe that good things are possible when you follow your heart. Your oath and intention are so powerful. Your personal declaration of will is the first step in a seemingly impossible journey. Now is the time for all humble, good-spirited servants, who believe that through love the world can be transformed into a sanctuary of abundance for all, to work together. The time has come.

The beginning of all change starts with your intention the very moment you choose to no longer accept the "reality" you see before you. Do not underestimate the power in an individual's commitment to harness the power of their intention, which is a way for all people to be powerful. Express your intentions now, and become the powerful change the world needs to be healed.

Declaration of Independence from Unrighteous Dominion

We submit to the whole and unimpeachable truth that all flesh and blood souls are sovereign entities, accountable only to their own consciences, and to the natural laws that envelop all creatures. Human law is NOT an extension of natural law, except where it is applied to oneself by oneself as free sentient beings, for the human domain is the domain of thought. Each person is endowed by these natural laws, with the unalienable right to seek their destiny in accord with the dictates of their consciences, limited only by the confines of the greater good of all.

Slaves are created with words, and so it is with words that we create, and set ourselves free. Accordingly, we find it necessary, in this era of subdued and abandoned personal freedom, to take back our power and to speak with one voice, to make a declaration of independence from all forms of foul dominion.

The power of nations comes from the people, and we, at any time, reserve the right to energetically revoke that power, reclaiming and marshaling for ourselves all power, except where, through consent of the people, we allow our energy to flow and join with others for the greater good, welfare, justice and protection of all.

We inviolably avow, concomitant with the obligations of defiance and defense, that we shall subordinate ourselves to no earthly masters, nor shall we seek mastery over others, nor stand idly by, as any vile usurper surreptitiously or overtly violates the freedom of another, or while innocence is victimized by cruelty.

Freedom is beyond the reach of any word, contract or compact, for people are creations of the universe, whose free will no power or entity can abate, as we are intrinsically empowered by the infinite nature of self-determination to choose our own path.

Predicated upon the unalterable truth of equality, the equal gift of life, and upon innate individual autonomy, and entitled to all of the powers and human rights that no entity can rightfully trespass upon, and deriving our individual powers from the same free-flowing source, from which all freedom springs, we hereby, make our declaration. We irrevocably proclaim ourselves to be an independent world of free people; a interconnected human family-state of universal citizens, called the human nation, existing within all nations as a united world family.

All souls seeking asylum find WITHIN the unimpeded path to your own freedom and destiny.

The Time for Revolution

"Civil disobedience becomes a sacred duty when the state has become lawless or corrupt. And a citizen who barters with such a state shares in its corruption and lawlessness."

—Gandhi

The human theater of conflict is a battle for hearts and minds through the world of symbols, words and ideas. This is because the rulers of the paper cities need your intention and your permission to exist. Countries, states, cities, corporations and laws are all words on paper. When the paper cities have become unjust prisons, we must revolt, and burn those paper cities to the ground. Then from the ashes, we must write new words for new generations. You are that generation. You are the author of the real-life story called, *tomorrow*. Unleash your mighty words, and with them, recreate a new and more beautiful world for all.

- We must each achieve greater individual consciousness and self-knowledge, and project mindful kindness toward everything and everyone.

- The revolution of consciousness is connected to the food revolution. As an organism, there is nothing more relevant or sacred than what you put into your body. Food is a part of our contract with life. Cultivate clarity, strength, vitality and power from natural, beautiful and organic living foods.

- We must remember that nature is the supreme cradle of life, and must be protected and treated with the highest respect and care.

- We must plant trees, grow gardens instead of lawns, ride bicycles when we can and support responsible local businesses over big brands.

- We must quit living vicariously through the fictional lives of TV and movie characters, and become the stars of our own real-life stories of adventure and creativity.

- We must quit thinking we know everything, and quit placing "knowledge" over kindness and compassion.

- We must reprogram ourselves to understand that cooperation is a higher principle than competition.

- We must strive for literacy and education that teach us to never quit questioning and probing at the assumptions of the day.

- We must understand that out of community and dialogue, the answers will arrive in their own time and way.

- We must question every inner-belief we possess without fear or attachment. Find comfort in questioning yourself. Criticism is no threat to your self-esteem or identity, but rather informs you.

- We must rebuild organic communities, where people can come together and have analogue conversations and share stories, art, music and emotions.

- We must relentlessly and unyieldingly protect freedom of speech and peaceful assembly.

- We must take the money out of politics, and end psychopathic, self destructive government and corporate madness.

- We must resist in-group thinking and practice seeing every soul as a brother or sister in a larger grouping of humans on earth.

- We must resist impulses to attack people, their credibility or their nature, and focus only on sharing our own positive creations, contributions, ideas and solutions.

- We must reject the artificial and embrace what is real and true: truth in food, community, relationships and self.

- We must step out of our digital avatars, and come together and have face-to-face dialogue as often as possible.

- We must remember that we cannot change others, we can only change ourselves.

- We must let our every act be out of love, and for the greater good of all.

- We must be our own authentically unique truth, and question who we are, what created us, and what processes within us are alien and externally created.

- We must share! Sharing IS caring. Share everything: every idea, every resource, every story, every gift, every worry and every burden. Share yourself.

- Above all we must be free, but to have real freedom, you must be wild and free yourself.

In a world of hate, love is the revolution. You reclaim your power by loving what you were once taught to hate. So, when is the time for revolt? The freest societies are in a constant state of revolution. The time for revolt is now, and the time for revolt is always! There is something beautiful in you seeking freedom. You are sufficient. It is sufficient to simply be a human being. Go within, seek yourself, know yourself and then share yourself. Please, be kind to one another and seek beauty in all you do.

Go now, and do what you can, and act always with the spirit of optimism, and always with love, and always for the greater good of all.

The *voice of reason* is speaking, and now is the time to listen.

The future depends on you...

A Request from the Author

After you read this book, please give it as a gift to someone. Freedom is a beautiful gift. If the paper continues to move from hand to hand, then the materials and the ideas are being recycled and reused.

Please send your blurbs and endorsements to publish here:
vor@bryantmcgill.com

Please leave comments on Amazon: (This Helps)
bryantmcgill.com/amazonvor

The book's official page is at:
bryantmcgill.com/vor

Some revolution quotes and reading lists are at:
bryantmcgill.com/revolution

For speaking, lectures, podcasts, radio or media interviews:
booking@bryantmcgill.com

You may find @bryantmcgill on his twitter account here:
twitter.com/bryantmcgill

For all other general information please visit:
bryantmcgill.com

Glossary

accost: to approach and speak to boldly or aggressively, as with a demand or request.

acquiescence: the reluctant acceptance of something without protest.

ambient: of or relating to the immediate surroundings of something.

ancillary: providing necessary support to the primary activities or operations of an organization, institution, industry or system; additional; subsidiary.

animus: from Latin animus ("the mind, in a great variety of meanings: the rational soul in man, intellect, consciousness, will, intention, courage, spirit, sensibility, feeling, passion, pride, vehemence, wrath, etc.; the breath, life, soul"), closely related to anima, which is a feminine form.

asceticism: the principles and practices of an ascetic; extreme self-denial and austerity. the doctrine that the ascetic life releases the soul from bondage to the body and permits union with the divine.

austerity: the quality of being austere; the trait of great self-denial (especially refraining from worldly pleasures); severe and rigid economy; reduced availability of luxuries and consumer goods.

authoritarian: characterized by or favoring absolute obedience to authority, as against individual freedom; favoring, denoting, or relating to government by a small elite with wide powers.

bellicose: demonstrating aggression and willingness to fight.

coercion: the practice of persuading someone to do something by using force or threats.

colloidal: of the nature of, relating to, or characterized by a colloid or colloids; particles of one substance dispersed through a second substance, where the particles do not settle and cannot be separated out by ordinary filtering or centrifuging like those in a suspension.

commensurate: corresponding in size or degree; in proportion.

commoditization: the action of turning something into or treating something as a (mere) commodity.

complex systems: Complex systems is a new approach to science that studies how relationships between parts give rise to the collective behaviors of a system and how the system interacts and forms relationships with its environment. [wikipedia]

concomitant: of a quality, circumstance, etc.; occurring along with something else, accompanying.

contrivance: a thing that is created skillfully and inventively to serve a particular purpose.

corporatization: to be influenced by or take on the features of a large commercial business, esp. in being bureaucratic and uncaring; the spread of corporate structure.

corporatocracies: describing a situation in which corporate bodies interact with sovereign power in an unhealthy alignment between business and political power. It describes an elite, sometimes termed the "1 percent," which maintains ties between business and government, sometimes by lobbying efforts or funding political advertising campaigns, or providing bailouts when corporations are seen as too big to fail, for the purpose of controlling government and dictating policy to serve its financial interests. [wikipedia]

coup d'état: a sudden, violent, and illegal seizure of power from a government.

decimate: kill, destroy, or remove a large percentage or part of; drastically reduce the strength or effectiveness of (something).

despot: a ruler or other person who holds absolute power, typically one who exercises it in a cruel or oppressive way.

dichotomous: a division or contrast between two things that are or are represented as being opposed or entirely different.

duopoly: a situation in which two suppliers dominate the market for a commodity or service.

dystopian: an imagined place or state in which everything is unpleasant or bad, typically a totalitarian or environmentally-degraded one.

economies of scale: the decrease in unit cost of a product or service resulting from large-scale operations, as in mass production.

ecumenical: promoting or relating to unity among the world's Christian churches.

egregious: outstandingly bad; shocking.

emergence: in philosophy, systems theory, science and art, emergence is the way complex systems and patterns arise out of a multiplicity of relatively simple interactions. Emergence is central to the theories of integrative levels and of complex systems.

epistemology: the branch of philosophy that studies the nature of knowledge, its presuppositions and foundations, and its extent and validity; the study or a theory of the nature and grounds of knowledge especially with reference to its limits and validity.

eviscerated: disembowel (a person or animal); deprive (something) of its essential content.

excitotoxins: a substance added to foods and beverages that literally stimulates neurons to death, causing brain damage of varying degrees; can be found in such ingredients as monosodium glutamate, aspartame, cysteine, hydrolyzed protein and aspartic acid.

expedient: (of an action) convenient and practical although possibly improper or immoral; (of an action) suitable or appropriate.

faux: made in imitation; artificial; not genuine; fake or false.

fiat currency: inconvertible paper money of no real value, made legal tender by Government decree; money declared by a government to be legal tender though it is not convertible into standard specie.

hegemony: leadership or dominance, esp. by one country or social group over others.

homogeneity: the quality of being similar or comparable in kind or nature; the quality of lacking diversity or variation (even to the point of boredom); a condition in which everything is regular and unvarying.

homogenization: to make homogeneous; of the same kind, nature, or character; alike, similar, congruous; consisting of parts or elements of the same kind; of uniform character throughout.

hubris: presumption; excessive pride or self-confidence.

iconography: the visual images, symbols or modes of representation collectively associated with a person, cult, or movement; as in the iconography of pop culture.

immane: existing or operating within; inherent.

imperialism: a policy of extending a country's power and influence through diplomacy or military force; chiefly historical rule by an emperor.

industrialization: is the process of social and economic change that transforms a human group from an agrarian society into an industrial one. It is a part of a wider modernization process, where social change and economic development are closely related with technological innovation, particularly with the development of large-scale energy and metallurgy production. It is the extensive organization of an economy for the purpose of manufacturing.

industrial revolution: the complex of radical socioeconomic changes that are brought about when extensive mechanization of production systems results in a shift from home-based hand manufacturing to large-scale factory production.

inviolably: to be kept sacred or free from attack; not to be infringed or dishonored; not yielding to force or violence; unable to be broken, forced, or injured.

inexorable: impossible to stop or prevent; (of a person) impossible to persuade by request or entreaty.

Kcitcl and Jodl: Wilhelm Keitel, Alfred Jodl were defendants of the Nuremberg Trials who unsuccessfully used the defense of "following orders" during their trials. They were both tried, sentenced to death and hanged as a war criminals.

leviathans: a very large aquatic creature, esp. a whale; a thing that is very large or powerful; an autocratic monarch or state.

madrasas: a building or group of buildings used for teaching Islamic theology and religious law, typically including a mosque.

maleficence: causing or capable of causing harm or destruction, esp. by supernatural means.

maraud: to rove and raid in search of plunder; to raid or pillage for spoils.

meme: an element of a culture or system of behavior that may be considered to be passed from one individual to another by nongenetic means, esp. imitation; an image, video, phrase, etc. that is passed electronically from one Internet user to another.

meta-: denoting a nature of a higher order or more fundamental kind, as metalanguage, metatheory; denoting position behind, at the back, or after.

modus operandi: a particular way or method of doing something, esp. one that is characteristic or well-established; the way something operates or works.

monoculture: a single, homogeneous culture without diversity or dissension; the cultivation of a single crop on a farm or in a region or country.

motley: a heterogeneous, often incongruous mixture of elements; having elements of great variety or incongruity; heterogeneous; having many colors; variegated; parti-colored.

myopic: nearsighted; lacking imagination, foresight, or intellectual insight.

narcissism: extreme selfishness, with a grandiose view of one's own talents and a craving for admiration, as characterizing a personality type.

nouveau: new, fashionable; new person, new thing; modern; up to date.

odious: arousing or meriting strong dislike, aversion, or intense displeasure.

oligarchists: a member of an oligarchy; any of a small group holding power in a state. also, an advocate or supporter of oligarchy.

oligarchy: a small group of people having control of a country, organization, or institution.

ollieism: a subordinate acting illegally or unethically to get a job done because he wants to please his boss.

paradox: a seemingly absurd or self-contradictory statement or proposition which when investigated or explained may prove to be well-founded or true; a phenomenon that exhibits some contradiction or conflict with preconceived notions of what is reasonable or possible; a person of perplexingly inconsistent life or behavior; a statement or tenet contrary to received opinion or belief, esp. one that is incredible, absurd, or fantastic.

plutocracies: government by wealth or by the wealthy; a ruling or influential class of wealthy people.

Posse Comitatus: a federal statute prohibiting use of the military in civilian law enforcement.

power of the situation: social psychology topic suggesting the powerful role that the situation can play in human behavior; relating to Milgram's obedience studies on personality and social psychology; relating to cognitive dissonance theory and the power of authority; also see Phil Zimbardo's Stanford Prison Experiment.

progenitors: a person or thing from which a person, animal or plant is descended or originates; an ancestor or parent; a person who originates an artistic, political, or intellectual movement.

progeny: a descendant or the descendants of a person, animal, or plant; offspring

proliferation: rapid increase in numbers; rapid reproduction of a cell, part, or organism; a large number of something.

promulgates: promote or make widely known (an idea or cause); put (a law or decree) into effect by official proclamation.

robber-baron: one of the American industrial or financial magnates of the late 19th century who became wealthy by unethical means, such as questionable stock-market operations and exploitation of labor; feudal lord who robbed travelers passing through his domain.

quasi: seemingly; apparently but not really; being partly or almost.

serfdom: the state or condition of a person in a condition of servitude or modified slavery, in which the powers of the master are more or less limited by law or custom; spec. a laborer not allowed to leave the land on which he works, a villein; an agricultural laborer bound under the feudal system to work on his lord's estate.

sovereignty: supreme power or authority; the supreme controlling power in a community not under monarchical government; absolute and independent authority of a state, community, etc.

status quo: the existing state of affairs, esp. regarding social or political issues.

Stockholm syndrome: feelings of trust or affection felt in certain cases of kidnapping or hostage-taking by a victim toward a captor.

stratification: the condition of being stratified; a layered configuration; formation or deposition of layers, as of rock or sediments.

surreptitiously: obtained by suppression of the truth or by fraudulent misrepresentation; acting stealthily or secretly; crafty, sly; by stealth or in secret; underhand, clandestine.

syncope: a cutting short of something; sudden cessation or interruption; fainting; temporary loss of consciousness caused by an insufficient flow of blood to the brain.

pseudo: not genuine; sham; false, counterfeit, pretended, spurious; intellectually or socially pretentious; insincere, affected; meaningless.

superannuated: belonging to a superannuation plan; obsolete through age or new technological or intellectual developments.

supremacism: a person who believes in the supremacy of a particular (specified) racial, social, etc., group; an advocate of the supremacy of a particular group, esp. one determined by race or sex.

sycophant: a servile or abject flatterer; an obsequious person, a toady; a person who acts obsequiously toward someone important in order to gain advantage.

transgenic: an organism whose genome has been altered by the transfer of a gene or genes from another species or breed; in industry they are used to produce a desired substance or quality.

ubiquitous: present, appearing, or found everywhere; omnipresent.

unadulterated: complete, sheer, utter; not mixed or diluted with any different or extra elements; complete and absolute.

unhomogenized: not having undergone homogenization; not purposefully made to being similar or comparable in kind or nature.

usurper: a person who usurps someone or something; esp. a person who unlawfully seizes another's position or authority.

vehemently: esp. of an utterance: very forcibly or passionately expressed; caused by or indicative of strong feeling or excitement; of an action: characterized by or performed with exceptional force or violence.

vicissitudes: change or mutability regarded as a natural process or tendency in human affairs; the fact or liability of change occurring in a specified thing or area; an instance of this; changes in circumstances; uncertainties or variations of fortune or outcome.

visceral: of or relating to the viscera: the visceral nervous system; relating to deep inward feelings rather than to the intellect.

vituperate: blame or insult (someone) in strong or violent language; blame, abuse, find fault with, in strong or violent language; vilify, revile.

xenophobia: a deep antipathy to foreigners or to foreign things; intense or irrational dislike or fear of people from other countries.